THE CONSERVATION ALTERNATIVE

Raymond F. Dasmann

International Union for The Conservation of Nature and Natural Resources (IUCN), Morges, Switzerland

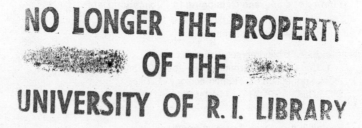

John Wiley & Sons, Inc. New York ▪ London ▪ Sydney ▪ Toronto

Photo Caption/Credit List

Chapter
    One   Coney Island, New York (Jan Lukas/Rapho Guillumette).
    Two   Water hole in South West Africa (F. Erize/Bruce Coleman).
  Three   Solar furnace, Font-Romeu, France (Claude Gazuit/Rapho Guillumette).
   Four   Auto junkyard (Bruce Roberts/Rapho Guillumette).
   Five   Industrial area of Kawasaki, Japan (Paolo Koch/Rapho Guillumette).
    Six   Afghanistan nomads (Marc Riboud/Magnum).
  Seven   Indians in upper Amazon basin (Cornell Capa/Magnum).
  Eight   Basque farm in Spain (Dorka Raynor/Nancy Palmer).

cover photo courtesy of NASA

Library of Congress Cataloging in Publication Data:

Dasmann, Raymond Frederick, 1919-
  The conservation alternative.

  Includes bibliographies and index.
  1. Conservation of natural resources. 2. Environmental protection. 3. Human ecology. I. Title.
S936.D28   301.31   74-34160
ISBN 0-471-19595-2

Printed in the United States of America

10 9 8 7 6 5 4 3 2 1

THE CONSERVATION ALTERNATIVE

Preface

This book will help students to obtain a quick grasp of the scope and significance of the environmental problems that confront humanity today. It is not intended to be comprehensive, and it will not take the place of a textbook on conservation. Many subjects of interest and importance are discussed only briefly. Instead, I emphasize the issues that must be given serious and immediate attention by everyone in the interests of human survival.

Since the last revision of my textbook, *Environmental Conservation,** I have attended international meetings in many countries and discussed the problems of human survival and human environment with people from many nations. It opened my eyes to matters that I should have been aware of long ago— particularly to the social changes that were started by the student movement of the 1960s and its successors. These things also brought about a loss of faith in the ability of the established institutions of technological society to respond to crises intelligently. However, they increased my faith in the ability of individuals to respond. Therefore, I expanded my area of inquiry to various works of social criticism, economic or political commentary, and psychological, religious, or cultural matters. Previously, many of these matters had seemed peripheral to a study of conservation. Instead, I have found that they are central, and that without considering this broader context there is no escape from our human and environmental dilemmas. Thus this book is broader in scope, although more restricted in detailed subject matter, than any of my previous work.

v

I have written this book with a sense of the overwhelming urgency of the situation confronting the human race. I hope that it will have an effect in bringing about the changes that are immediately essential. I cannot pretend to have answers to the problems confronting humanity, but I have pointed out the directions in which we must look to find them.

Although I indicate in the book that we are now heading into a series of minor and major catastrophes, I do not share the "doomsday" outlook. I have seen too many people change completely in their viewpoint and direction to doubt the ability of women and men to break loose from the bonds imposed by tradition and culture. I hope that we are seeing the emergence of a new breed of people, capable of understanding their own nature and, through this, its relationship with the whole of nature.

When anyone departs from areas of special competency there is a risk of error. My reviewers and editors have done their best to eliminate mistakes and irrationalities, but the ultimate responsibility is mine. I have done the best I could do at this time, and hope it is adequate.

Raymond F. Dasmann

Morges, Switzerland, 1974

Environmental Conservation, Third Edition, Wiley, 1972.

Acknowledgments

Much of the research, many of the better ideas, and considerable hard work was contributed by Elizabeth Dasmann who, nevertheless, declined coauthorship. Three young women—Sandra, Marlene, and Laurien—are jointly responsible for having "changed my head," after years of fruitless effort, to allow new ideas to filter in.

For inspiration and encouragement I am indebted to Peter Berg and Gary Snyder with whom I have discussed various ideas included here. The first draft of this book provided subject matter for a workshop at Michigan State University, organized by Professor Georg Borgstrom and attended by Shri Chandrasekhar, Gerald Leach, Nicholas Oteino, and various members of the Michigan State faculty. The consensus at this meeting agreed with the main thrust of this book. Most of the topics will be discussed at the triennial Technical Meeting of the International Union for the Conservation of Nature and Natural Resources (IUCN) to be held in Kinshasha, Zaire, in September 1975. I do not suggest that any of the people mentioned endorsed the conclusions reached here, nor that the book reflects the official views of IUCN—but I am grateful to all for their encouragement.

I could not have written this book without the continuing effort of Robert L. Rogers, who has the editorial responsibility for it.

R.F.D.

Contents

chapter one

Present Trends Cannot Continue

"The question remains open: which will ecology be, the last of the old sciences or the first of the new?"

Theodore Roszak, *Where the wasteland ends*

In the middle 1970s the human race is being forced to some critical decisions. We can try to continue with business as usual, to pursue goals of economic growth and material progress without concern for long-term consequences, or we can change direction. If we go on as before we will have at most a few more decades before serious breakdowns of civilization take place. Before that time there will be recurring and increasing catastrophes affecting great numbers of people. These have already begun. However, if we start now to change our course, while we still have relatively abundant supplies of energy and raw materials, we can develop ways of living on this planet that can be sustained, not just for decades but for thousands of years.

The coming years are totally without precedent in human history. Within the lifetimes of those who are still young decisions must be made that will determine whether civilized humanity will have a future. There is no option left to postpone the day of reckoning, or to pass today's problems on to posterity. If the wrong direction is taken there may well be no posterity.

1

We are caught in a major crisis of the human environment, and all other crises that may be described are related to it. Energy, food, poverty, population, the destruction of nature, and the breakdown of democratic societies are all facets of one central issue—how are we going to adjust our numbers, and the demands we make on the resources and living space of our planet to insure the long-term survival of the human race, and of the natural world on which we depend?

This book will attempt to clarify the fact that our current practices in relation to our use of energy, raw materials, the production of food, our continuing pollution of the earth, and our treatment of nature cannot continue. It will explore and seek to develop a conservation alternative to the existing ways of technological societies, an alternative built on the knowledge of the past and the techniques of the present and foreseeable future. I do not pretend to have any sudden insight that permits me to point the way out of the man-environment dilemma. Scarcely any of the ideas and material presented here are new. For more than a century, conservation-minded people have been calling attention to the things that must be done if the story of man on earth is not to be brought to a sudden and sad ending. Their advice generally has been ignored. But anyone who hopes to see the twenty-first century dawn can no longer afford such ignorance.

Conservation is both a point of view and a necessary line of action concerning the environment and its inhabitants. Its field includes all aspects of human existence. It necessarily must call into question the activities of governments, groups, and individuals. It must ask questions about the behavior and motivation of people, and about ways of life and institutions concerning which many would prefer to have no questions asked. A conservation viewpoint must challenge the right of human institutions and individuals to engage in activities that impair the long-term well being of other humans, other species, or the environments on which they all depend.

The conservation movement as a social force had its origins in the United States with a concern for the future of wild places and wild animal life. It now appears that it must make its final stand also in the United States. This country is in the strongest position to make the major changes that must come. It alone has both the physical capacity to change course without a total disruption of its economy and society, and a strong force of people who are deeply concerned with environmental issues.

A movement that originally started with a concern for wild nature may not seem a sufficient base on which to build a reorganization of society. But a movement that grants to wild nature a right to continued coexistence with humanity, and states that such a right takes precedence in at least some times and places over the desire of people to increase their share of worldly goods, has already challenged the premises on which an economy dedicated to continuing growth operates.

Admittedly, many who first acted to save wildlife and wild places saw no conflict between their interests and the continued growth and expansion of the national economy. In an America with great open spaces and few people there was originally little need for such conflict. But the conservation challenge was recognized by some of the movement's pioneers. Henry David Thoreau not only proclaimed that "In wildness is the preservation of the world," but recognized that man must be considered as "an inhabitant, or a part and parcel of Nature, rather than a member of society." He himself was in frequent opposition to the established order of his day, and insisted that a sane man must retain his obedience to "yet more sacred laws" even though these put him in conflict with the "most sacred laws of society."

Nineteenth-century America was intent, however, on following the biblical injunction in increase, multiply, and subdue the earth. It was at war with, and intent on conquering nature. Thoreau's view of man as a "part and parcel of Nature" was not reconcilable with the consciousness of his time. The slaughter of the buffalo, the destruction of the Indians, and the rape of the American west had scarcely begun. Yet there were those who listened to Thoreau, and as their strength grew they took the actions needed to slow down, and in places to halt, the despoliation of the land and its resources.

Full recognition of man as a part of nature, inseparable from his environment, was to follow with the development of the science of ecology, and the pursuit of ecological knowledge was to reveal the existence of those "yet more sacred laws" that must take precedence over mere human regulations. It falls on conservationists to call for a reorganization of human societies to bring them in balance with the realities of the earth on which they depend.

The words of conservationists, no matter how well spoken, have shaken no empires thus far, and have caused no worry among those who attempt to control the economic and political destiny of nations. Unlike the words of Marx or Lenin, they inspire no violent revolution. Yet they are equally revolutionary, and if humanity is to survive they must be heard now.

A Difference in Point of View

There are two things of fundamental importance to all people. One is to stay alive. The second is the quality of that existence. The second only comes into play when the first is provided for—a person dying of thirst will drink first and only later wonder if the water were polluted. To stay alive one must breathe air, drink water, eat, and keep one's body temperature relatively constant. In primitive times, in a favorable environment, one could meet those needs with relatively little effort. Under less favorable circumstances the process of keeping alive required constant, and sometimes desperate, effort. In modern civilization the basic needs remain the same, but the means for satisfying them are less obvious. For urban dwellers the activities required to obtain food, water, a dwelling place, clothing, and fresh air often seem little related to the needs to be satisfied. The complex activities required to keep a city population alive often defy the understanding of most people, including some who bear principal responsibility for carrying them out.

Over most of the world in the 1970s most people are mainly concerned with keeping themselves alive, and not much interested in the possible effects that their efforts may have on the world around them. A minority of the world's people, having been assured, at least for the present, of a continuing supply of necessities, give their time and energy to questions concerning the future, to the survival of the biosphere and its inhabitants, and to the quality of the environment in which they live. It follows that there is a difference in viewpoint between these two groups that leads to breakdowns in communication and understanding.

The peasant in a tropical country may have a principal concern for acquiring enough land to grow his food and will not comprehend anyone who objects to his cutting down the last tract of forest in order to obtain this land. He may willingly eat the last antelope that had survived in the forest, or kill the last leopard and sell its skin. Therein lies the basis for some of the most severe problems of the environment. A special responsibility rests on those who have money, education, and resources to find ways in which others who struggle for sheer survival can live without destroying the environment on which they must depend. Particularly, those who are more fortunate in material possessions must ascertain that their own demands do not create conditions that force others to take such dangerous measures.

Some Definitions

The term *environment,* as used in this book, refers to the biosphere, the ecosystems of which it is composed, and the modifications of these brought about by human action. The *biosphere* is now defined as the thin layer of soil, rock, water, and air that surrounds planet earth along with the living organisms for which it provides support, and which in turn modify it in directions that either enhance or lessen its life-supporting capacity. Although we are all part of the biosphere and are supported by it, we are seldom aware of its presence, and indeed much of it is beyond the reach of our senses. Therein lies one of the difficulties in making people aware of the reality of an environmental crisis. Relative to the total size of the planet, the biosphere is a shallow layer of air, water, soil, and rock not much more than 15 miles in depth measured from the bottom of the ocean to the highest point in the atmosphere at which life can survive without man-made protective devices. Furthermore, the biosphere appears to be unique to planet earth, although we may hope someday to find other biospheres and other forms of life somewhere in the universe (Unesco, 1970).

Ecosystems are subdivisions of the biosphere and consist of communities of plants, animals, and microorganisms along with the air, water, soil, or other substrate that supports them. Ecosystems and the biosphere are powered by energy, most of which is derived directly or indirectly from sunlight. A pond and the environment that surrounds it is an example of an ecosystem. So also is a forest and its surrounding environment, or a meadow with its supporting air, soil, and water. Ecosystems vary from very simple—for example, a community of lichens growing on rocks in the high Arctic—to very complex, such as coral reef communities in tropical seas, tropical rain forests, or modern cities (Fraser Darling and Dasmann, 1969).

The term *conservation* has had many meanings during its history of use, but is now taken to mean *the rational use of the environment to provide the highest sustainable quality of living for humanity*. Like all brief definitions this one needs explanation. *Rational use* implies both the protection and management of the environment and its natural resources with a view to maintain a suitable habitat for humanity and for other living creatures for the longest foreseeable period of time. *Quality of living* includes the fulfillment of man's quantitative needs for survival, but beyond that it includes the availability of rich and diverse habitats able to satisfy the wants and aspirations of the great diversity of human beings that exist on earth. It necessarily involves an environment free from harmful levels of pollutants injurious to life. It also involves an environment capable of supporting the widest possible variety of other forms of life, wild or domestic. No two people will agree on the factors that contribute most toward their view of "quality of living." It is a goal of conservation to keep the options open in the environment, so that the widest diversity of views and life styles can be accommodated.

To be successful, conservation must be based on an understanding of *ecology,* which is defined as that science concerned with the interrelationships among living things and with the nonliving environment. Ecology is not a new science. The word was first coined by Ernst Haeckel, a German biologist, in 1869. But ecological studies had been carried out before Haeckel's time, for example, by Alexander von Humboldt in the latter part of the eighteenth century (Odum, 1971). Even in Greek and Roman antiquity ecological ideas were understood and ecological investigations were carried out. It could be argued that the earliest people were ecologically oriented and very concerned with understanding their relationships with other species and with the environments that they occupied (Glacken, 1967).

Insofar as its effects on public thinking and action are concerned, ecology is a latecomer in the scientific world, following behind astronomy, physics, chemistry, genetics, taxonomy, or medical science. Whereas most sciences have proceeded by a reductive, analytic method, separating complex phenomena into simple components and then investigating those components, ecology at its best is an integrative, synthesizing science concerned with the operation of total living systems and proceeds by bringing together knowledge from a number of related disciplines. Therefore, ecology has been something of a maverick among sciences, and the ecologist has at times been looked down upon by his scientific colleagues as being "not quite one of the elect" scientific fraternity. However, in the face of serious troubles with the human environment, the ecologist has gained recognition.

The "environment movement," the "ecology movement," and the "conservation movement" are considered here to be the same. Of the three the term "conservation movement" has been in use for the longest period of time. In its earlier days conservation had a more limited definition and a narrower range of concerns. However, as conservation came to be based on an understanding of ecology its scope broadened to take in the entire human environment. Conservation writers from George Perkins Marsh (1864) to William Vogt (1948), Fairfield Osborn (1949), and Aldo Leopold (1948) tended to be as broadly "environmental" in their concerns as are the environmentalists of the 1960s and 1970s.

Ecology as a scientific discipline is bound by its own rules. It produces information on which action may be based. For conservation, one takes this knowledge, places it within a framework of human values, and proceeds to action. Conservation has been a growing social force, and until the time when the activities and attitudes that it calls for become an accepted part of human existence, conservation will remain a necessary social force on which the continued survival of humanity will depend. There is no question of the conservation movement or of the "environment thing" dying out as a passing fad. Until the real and serious problems of the environment are solved, it must and will remain.

The definition of conservation presented here is not necessarily accepted everywhere, nor are the implications of conservation that are discussed in this book necessarily recognized even by some of the most active conservationists. To many, and particularly those who derive their wealth from the exploitation of natural resources, a restricted definition of conservation is preferred. Conservation may be considered by some of these merely as a form of good behavior in the out-of-doors: don't start forest fires (and burn up my timber), do carry out those activities that lead to greater productivity (and increase my profits), help prevent floods (and keep my farm from washing away). Conservation in this sense is *wise use,* with the emphasis on *use.* This practical view of conservation colored the words of those who first used the term "conservation" in America—Gifford Pinchot (1947) and Theodore Roosevelt (Nash, 1968). Forests were protected because they would yield wood, water supply, and the like for man's use. Wildlife was protected so that man could later hunt it or make use of it in some other direct way.

But other pioneers in the conservation field viewed things differently. Thoreau was not use oriented—he wanted to protect nature for its own sake and for the joy of having wild things around. John Muir (1901), California's pioneer conservationist, devoted his latter years to battling the Roosevelt-Pinchot school of thinking in an effort to prevent the building of Hetchy-Hetchy Dam in Yosemite National Park.

What has been called the "preservationist" school of conservation may favor nonuse, except for those activities believed not to interfere with or impair natural processes. Their opposition is not to use, but to consumptive use, which involves the removal or drastic alteration of plant or animal life. In a world where wild things grow more scarce, they favor protection and preservation of wild species and places, avoiding their exploitation while usually allowing their availability to people who seek inspiration and recreation from them. This opposition to consumptive use is generally restricted to the application of such use to natural areas of high inspirational or recreational value, or to wildlife. It is not opposition to the production of necessary resources from other areas.

The adherents of these two points of view tend to annoy one another and to engage in caustic criticisms of each other's viewpoints. Those who attempt to mediate between them are likely to win no more gratitude than the person who breaks up a dogfight. But conservation is both wise use and preservation, and much more. It is far more deeply involved in the most basic and controversial issues of modern society than would appear on the surface.

The conservation movement has had its greatest growth during the late 1960s and early 1970s, although more is now demanded. This growth took place not only because of the serious state of environmental affairs, which seemed to be growing less tolerable, but also because the observable trends affecting the environment seemed to head toward catastrophe. Nevertheless, the degree of environmental concern probably would not have developed had there not also been a "crisis of confidence" in the institutions of government and economy that had been relied on to provide increasing wealth and well being for all. The late 1960s and early 1970s have been a period of social change, verging on revolution, throughout the world. The spirit of unrest in America was spurred by racial injustice, the Indochina Wars, the continued denial of an equal place for women in society, the restrictive world view provided by science and technology that seemed to leave less and less room for the human spirit, and the continuance of outmoded sexual and behavioral injunctions (Reich, 1971; Roszak, 1968). This atmosphere of change and revolt soon encompassed the environmental concerns that had previously been the preoccupation of conservation groups who had little public support. With the sudden influx of enthusiastic supporters, the environment movement became a potent political force.

The Environmental Crisis

The crisis of the human environment has been built up by the interaction of a number of different factors, of which four major groupings can be described: population, pollution, technological growth, and land use. Each of these acting separately might not be sufficient to warrant the term "crisis." Converging as they do in a limited biosphere they give rise to a situation that holds the threat of disaster, and a guarantee of continuing "minor" catastrophes until the situation has been corrected.

Population.   With the numbers of people on earth rapidly approaching four billion, at a growth rate that remains almost 2 percent per year, a condition of overpopulation exists. This overpopulation is either absolute, meaning that a decrease to a lower level must be accomplished before the symptoms can be relieved (and this is arguable) or it is at least relative (which is undeniable) meaning that the numbers of people are too great for existing social, economic, and political structures to provide for their well being. The numbers of people on earth are now so high that only a minority receives an adequate share of the earth's resources to maintain a reasonable level of physical well being (Borgstrom, 1965). Even this minority finds that the quality of life is impaired by the presence of excessive numbers, whereas the majority find it difficult to stay alive. As these words are being written millions of people are on the verge of starvation in the Saharan-Sahelian region of North Africa, and even greater numbers are being threatened in Bangladesh and India.

Nevertheless, it is not so much the actual numbers of people that create a crisis situation as the rate of growth, which, *if it were to continue,* would cause a doubling of numbers in 35 years, and so on to another doubling, and another. Consider that existing levels of population continue in a state of strife, conflict, and an unacceptable level of human suffering, the prospect of greater numbers can only cause grave concern. Particularly distressing is the distribution of population in relation to the availability of natural resources and advanced technology, which results in a division of the world into rich nations and poor nations. The continuing conflict between the two for a fair distribution of the earth's resources will accelerate with the increasing population.

Obviously this condition cannot continue. Populations cannot go on doubling and redoubling. Growth will cease. The question to be answered is when? If growth continues for much longer it will be brought to a halt by a growing death rate. This is the hard way to go. It makes far more sense and is more humane to decrease the birth rate. For some countries this is difficult because the people do not understand the problem. For others, such as the United States, a decrease could be accomplished, and is being accomplished. There is no great mystery about what it takes to bring population growth to a halt. Zero population growth could be accomplished in the United States next year if the women of the country decided to produce children only in a number equal to the number of people who would be expected to die in that year from all causes. It could be done, but will it?

Pollution.   Pollution of the environment has concerned mankind since people first came together in villages and cities. Initially the main problem involved the disposal or proper use of human wastes and other forms of organic garbage. In most of the poor countries of the world this kind of pollution still remains the most serious and difficult problem to deal with. Failure to handle the organic waste situation in a rational way produces conditions under which diseases are cultured and spread. Cholera, amoebic dysentery, typhoid, and other fatal or debilitating diseases spread quickly among people who have inadequate sanitation, and other diseases such as typhus and bubonic plague are spread by rodents that thrive in areas where human wastes and garbage are allowed to accumulate. The pollution of soil, water, and living space by organic wastes is of great worldwide consequence, and in those countries where systems for the disposal or use of sewage do not exist the problem increases with growing populations (Unesco, 1970).

Despite the seriousness of the problems involving sewage and garbage, it is other types of pollutants that contribute most strongly to a pollution crisis. These are the chemicals produced by technologically advanced societies and associated with urban-industrial communities. Some of these are substances that would normally be present in the environment, but in lesser amounts, such as heavy metals, or the products resulting from the incomplete combustion of coal or petroleum that contribute most heavily to urban air pollution, or petroleum itself when it is spread on the oceans. Others are new chemicals synthesized in laboratories and not normally present in nature—the various organic pesticides and herbicides, the PCBs (polychlorinated biphenyls) used in some industries, and certain radioactive materials. These are toxic in varying degrees to many or all forms of life.

With growing populations, with the need to increase food output from agricultural lands, with the expansion and increase in industrial production, the poisoning of the environment, or the disruption of chemical balances in the environment in directions that are undesirable will grow. The means for controlling pollution are available. For some pollutants, however, the costs of control can mean higher prices for the products of industry and agriculture and these can be particularly damaging to people in the poor countries of the world.

There are ways out of this dilemma, but with continuing population growth and technological growth, they can be difficult to put into practice. However, continued increase in levels of pollution *cannot* be tolerated. Whatever disruptions may be caused in order to bring pollution under control *must* be tolerated (Leonard, 1972).

Technological Growth. The word "technology" is variously defined, but if we accept the dictionary definition it is "the totality of the means employed to provide objects necessary for human sustenance and comfort." Therefore, it has been a necessary part of human life from the beginning. The advanced technology of the twentieth century, however, is of a different order from those technologies that have preceded it. Lewis Mumford (1966) has noted this difference as follows: "The last century, we all realize, has witnessed a radical transformation of the entire human environment, largely as a result of the impact of the mathematical and physical sciences upon technology. This shift from an empirical, tradition-bound technics to an experimental mode has opened up such realms as those of nuclear energy, supersonic transportation, cybernetic intelligence and instantaneous distant communication." The growth of this technology, based on the application of science and mathematics to industrial processes, had its start in Europe but has now spread worldwide. With its existing massive size and rate of growth it is a dominant force in the biosphere compared to which nation-states and international organizations appear as mere adjuncts. It exists in the communist and capitalist world and dominates the daily life of all people caught up in its network, and few today are not.

Writing of the new "technological society," Jacques Ellul (1969) has pointed out that "Technique requires predictability and, no less, exactness of prediction. It is necessary, then, that technique prevail over the human being. For technique, this is a matter of life and death. Technique must reduce man to a technical animal, the king of the slaves of technique."

Describing the new "technocracy" Theodore Roszak (1968) defines it as "that society in which those who govern justify themselves by appeal to technical experts who, in turn, justify themselves by appeal to scientific forms of knowledge. And beyond the authority of science, there is no appeal." Further, he states: ". . . technocracy easily eludes all traditional political categories. Indeed it is characteristic of the technocracy to render itself ideologically invisible."

Lewis Mumford (1966) has warned that "With this new 'megatechnics' the dominant minority will create a uniform, all-enveloping, super-planetary structure, designed for automatic operation. Instead of functioning actively as an autonomous personality, man will become a passive, purposeless, machine-conditioned animal. . . ."

The significance, growth, and control of technology are of central concern to conservation. The dynamic force of economic growth and development has shown itself capable of overriding all other human considerations. The pursuit of the dream of increased technological efficiency with the expected gain in forms of material wealth has led to the blotting out of landscapes, human communities, and the destruction of species and resources that could have been protected if more human values had prevailed. Particularly relevant to conservation is the demand on material resources: the metals, minerals, and other things that technology requires as the raw materials of manufacturing, and on energy resources. Nations with advanced technologies such as the United States, Canada, Japan, and the nations of Europe, although they possess a minority of the world's population, consume the greater part of the world's mineral and energy resources. Serious questions have been raised about the capacity of all known or predictable sources of supply of minerals or energy to support such high rates of consumption. It is virtually certain that the resources cannot be found, or put into use, that will support all the people of the world at the rates of energy and material consumption that have characterized the United States. Thus, if the so-called "high standard of living" characteristic of the United States represents a goal toward which all people strive, that goal cannot be reached (Meadows et al., 1972). This creates not only an environmental crisis but, in a sense, a world revolutionary condition that is more far-reaching than has before been envisioned. This means a condition in which the continuance of existing social, economic, and political forms is not only intolerable but impossible (Roszak, 1972).

Land Use.   Before there were serious problems concerning population, pollution, or advanced technology, there were great difficulties involving land use. Worldwide these problems are now of such a serious character that they demand immediate attention. Land-use problems include the misuse of land and its living resources leading to its degradation, the destruction of species, and ultimately the total loss of its productive capacity. In all the old centers of civilization, in the Mediterranean region, the Middle East, India, or Latin America, we find evidence of past misuse of land. This may be in the form of desert-like conditions in lands that were once capable of high productivity. It may be seen in the disappearance of ancient cities under drifting sand or dust, or in the silt deposited by rivers that once ran clear. One sees the evidence in the encroachment of scrub and jungle over agricultural lands that once supported the old Amerindian centers of civilization, and in mountains where only bare rocks remain in place of once carefully terraced fields.

Misuse of land and of its living resources continues. It occurs among primitive peoples whose numbers have increased and whose space has diminished so that old methods of shifting agriculture can no longer maintain the land. It occurs among pastoralists who crowd too many grazing animals into too small a space and in consequence replace productive grasslands with barren wastes. It occurs in the spread of cities over the most fertile farmland, or in the blotting out of rich and teeming coastal estuaries by urban development. Great areas of the most productive tropical forests are destroyed each year to make room for temporary pastures, or transient and low-yielding agriculture. Whole mountains are destroyed by strip mining and left as stark monuments to human greed. Scenic wildernesses supporting thousands of living species are blotted out to provide a small financial gain for a few people.

Misuse of land took place when human populations were sparse, and it remains an important factor even in the less densely populated regions of the world. However, when people are few land can be left to recover. As human populations increase and the pressures on all land are intensified, the opportunity for the repair of damaged land by natural processes disappears. The crisis of land use thus intersects with the other major pressures on the human environment to create an ever-growing and total environmental crisis.

Ways Out?

If there were easy answers to environmental problems we would no doubt have found them long ago and put them into application. But what is needed will affect all of man's activities and attitudes. Since it has seemed unlikely that people will accept the changes that are necessary, many environmentalists have appeared as "prophets of doom." Defeatist attitudes, however, can be harmful, since they can result in a failure to take even the most obvious and necessary steps to improve the situation. Furthermore, humanity has shown itself to be capable, from time to time, of accepting drastic changes in attitudes, behavior and actions. Such changes are now needed.

There seems little doubt that humanity itself must take on the responsibility for reorganizing its use of lands and natural resources in order to guarantee their continued availability and productivity. There is no doubt that people every-where must accept the need to limit their own reproduction to achieve not only "zero population growth" but, for some areas at least, a period of popula-tion decline, if we are to achieve human freedom in a world of natural abun-dance. There is no doubt that changes in attitude toward so-called "rights" to misuse land and mistreat our fellow travellers on "spaceship earth" must be brought about. There is no doubt that major political, social, and economic changes that will lead to the emergence of a different, more sane, humane, and considerate world must take place. The truth of these statements will be examined in the chapters that follow.

It is essential to examine the goals toward which conservation must strive even at the risk of offending many conservationists. The conservation move-ment has traditionally aspired toward limited goals and has not looked at the implications of their achievements. It is one thing to fight to protect the local marsh from pollution, but quite another to recognize the right of all people everywhere to protect their local marshes from pollution. Yet, if conservation is to have any acceptable rationale, and any degree of logical consistency, the broad implications of the goals sought, and actions directed toward their achievement, must be recognized.

The conservation movement seeks to change the world from what it has become under the past impact of civilization to what it might be under more enlightened management. It is essential to examine its aims and to explore their implications from an ecological and social viewpoint. The kind of world that conservationists must strive to achieve is therefore stated to be one in which:

1. *At least a minimum means for survival is provided for all people.*   This means that each person, at birth, must be granted the right to the means by which he can obtain food, clothing, fresh air, fresh water, living space, and fuel sufficient to enable him to survive. This does not mean that a long life span can be guaranteed for anyone, since this is not humanly possible

within the vagaries of human genetics and the nature of the biosphere. It does mean a guaranteed means for earning an income, or a guarantee of sufficient land and living space to sustain life.

2. *All individuals are free to choose a life style that is personally accepta-ble and that does not seriously abridge the rights of others.* To take ex-tremes, this means the right of some people, and not necessarily "primitives," to a hunting-fishing-food gathering way of life, of others to a life of pastoral nomadism, of still others to a high technology (to the extent that this can be achieved) with the prospect of travel to the stars. Many variants and intrica-cies of life styles lie between these extremes.

Without such provisions, conservation remains a game played by the world's elite without the support of the less privileged. Or conservation gains can be made by those who hold power in a nation-state through the suppression of cultural minorities or at their expense. But the power of the elite diminishes daily, and the dominant ethnic group of today may be tomorrow's oppressed minority. Conservation must be a concern of all the people if it is to succeed.

3. *All species are assured a continued coexistence with humanity on plan-et earth, to the extent that mankind can provide such assurance.* This in-cludes a minimum guarantee of living space in a suitable habitat for each species, and the absence in that living space of levels of man-made pollution damaging to the species concerned. This is the only provision of the three that can be considered a traditional conservation goal. Although no less impor-tant than the other two, it can be realized in the long run, only if the preceding provisions are put into effect. Otherwise the individual's prerogative to seek his personal well being will take precedence over the survival of both the natu-ral world and the human race.

These three declarations, while easy enough to state, affect all aspects of human life. They require, at a minimum, the cessation of continued increase in human numbers. Even the first of these provisions cannot be arranged at present levels of human population and social organization. Provision of the second and third rights requires at least a redistribution of populations and for some areas a reduction in human numbers. Thus, achievement of these aims involves a duty for individuals to restrict their reproduction to a level that will not result in continuing population growth.

Achievement of these aims further challenges the concept of national sover-eignty, which at present allows any nation to pursue whatever course it chooses within its own boundaries. It disputes the authority of individuals or families in feudal economies, of individuals, groups, or corporations in capitalist econo-mies, or of state organizations in socialist economies to carry out exploitation of land, natural resources, or human beings beyond levels acceptable to the total world community. This in turn could call for some type of world organiza-tion that can guarantee the rights of species and of human individuals, and that can prevent wars or other forms of coercion on the part of nations or groups within the world community. Alternatively it may call for the abolition of all nations or centralized power structures.

If one accepts these aims as representing the goals toward which we must strive, how does one get there from here? What is the responsibility of a nation that reaches a level of environmental and human sanity toward those nations that continue to allow unlimited population increase and exploitation of resources beyond levels that could have worldwide acceptance? How does the world community enforce its will on a nation that refuses to accept the rights of individuals, peoples, or species, and insists, for example, in carrying out an insane destructive war against another nation?

It may be that the goals expressed are unreachable. We may prove to be like the moth in the James Thurber fable who insisted on flying toward a star instead of following the example of his fellow moths who flew into the nearest candle. When interviewed later he admitted that he had not yet reached the star, but on the other hand he had lived to be a very old and wise moth. If there are better and more realizable goals, they should be expressed. But we cannot continue to follow the self-destructive goals that humanity has thus far pursued.

The absence of defined and understood goals has been one of the principal causes of human confusion and environmental degradation. It is better to subscribe to a view of conservation that calls for a total transformation of human attitudes and behavior, and can thereby succeed, than to follow halfheartedly a view that seems broadly acceptable because it is generally confused. The greatest danger that conservationists face is the trap that Aldo Leopold (1948) once described, where in our effort to make conservation easy we make it trivial.

References

Borgstrom, Georg. 1965. *The hungry planet*. Macmillan, New York.

Ellul, Jacques. 1964. *The technological society*. A.A. Knopf, New York.

Fraser Darling, Frank, and R.F. Dasmann. 1969. The ecosystem view of human society. *Impact of Science on Society*. Unesco, Paris, *19*: 109–122.

Glacken, Clarence. 1967. *Traces on the Rhodian shore*. University of California Press, Berkeley.

Leonard, George. 1972. *The transformation. A guide to the inevitable changes in humankind*. Delacorte Press, New York.

Leopold, Aldo. 1948. *A sand county almanac*. Oxford, New York.

Marsh, George Perkins. 1864. *Man and nature; or, physical geography as modified by human action*. Scribners, New York.

Meadows, D.H., et al. 1972. *The limits to growth*. New American Library, New York.

Muir, John. 1901. *Our national parks*. Houghton, Boston.

Mumford, Lewis. 1966. *The myth of the machine. Technics and human development.* Harcourt Brace, New York.

Nash, Roderick. 1968. *The American environment.* Addison-Wesley, Reading, Mass.

Odum, Eugene P. 1971. *Fundamentals of ecology.* W.B. Saunders, Philadelphia. 3rd edition.

Osborn, Fairfield. 1949. *Our plundered planet.* Little Brown, Boston.

Pinchot, Gifford. 1947. *Breaking new ground.* Harcourt, Brace and World, New York.

Reich, Charles A. 1971. *The greening of America.* Bantam Books, New York.

Roszak, Theodore. 1968. *The making of a counterculture.* Faber and Faber, London (1971 ed).

Roszak, Theodore. 1972. *Where the wasteland ends. Politics and transcendence in postindustrial society.* Doubleday, New York.

Thoreau, Henry David. 1893. *Excursions, the writings of Henry David Thoreau.* Riverside ed., Boston, 11 Volume IX: 251.

Thoreau, Henry David. 1960. *Walden or Life in the Woods, and On the Duty of Civil Disobedience* (with an afterword by Perry Miller). New American Library, New York.

Unesco. 1970. *Use and conservation of the biosphere.* Natural Resources Research X, Unesco, Paris.

Vogt, William. 1948. *Road to survival.* William Sloane, New York.

chapter two

Some Rules of the Game

"The hostile attitude of conquering nature ignores the basic interdependence of all things and events—that the world beyond the skin is actually an extension of our own bodies—and will end in destroying the very environment from which we emerge and upon which our whole life depends."

Alan Watts, *The book on the taboo against knowing who you are*

Humanity inherited a world of untold richness and diversity, and for hundreds of thousands of years formed a part of this world, modifying and shaping it in places to suit human ends, but not subtracting from its wealth or variety. This benign state of affairs started to unravel in some parts of the world a few thousand years ago. The concentration of people into city civilizations created a condition of stress between man and nature, a separation between the human and the natural world. To survive, these centers needed to channel more and more of the flow of energy and materials into directions thought more suitable to human purposes. Faced with the tangled and infinitely complex networks that characterize the natural world, they began to organize, straighten out, and to discard those pieces that seemed unnecessary. Diversity was simplified, variety made uniform.

17

But for thousands of years civilized humanity was protected from its lack of understanding by its lack of power. Walking on foot or travelling by horseback, carried by the strength of oars or the power of wind in the sails, people could reach all parts of the world—but slowly. With muscle power, horse power, or ox power they could move mountains and build pyramids—but slowly. With spears and swords, bows and arrows, traps and snares they could destroy or capture animals that seemed dangerous, competitive, or useful, and they did, but only a few. In the meanwhile there was time to learn.

Only a couple of centuries ago time suddenly began to run out. New sources of power were tapped, power that had been locked in the earth a half-billion years or more, since the swamp forests of an ancient era were compacted into coal, and the teeming life of early oceans was transformed into petroleum or natural gas. With these fossil fuels and the machines that could transform their energy into work, there came the capacity for rapid change and quick destruction.

Far too soon in relation to any development of human understanding, a still greater source of power was discovered. When the first nuclear blasts shook the world, humanity was on its way to share the power that fires the sun. With this new source of energy the human race has started to remodel the world. Regrettably for all forms of life, we do not know what we are doing, and we have lost the time to contemplate quietly the significance of our past actions.

The tragedy of today's people is that the physical increase in human power has not been accompanied by the needed increase in self-understanding, through which could come understanding of our fellow creatures on earth. The development of self, and the accompanying development of life-respecting behavior, has lost the race against an accelerating technology. In a nuclear age we possess, at best, a stone-age psychology. We retain a willingness to win arguments by clubbing our opponent into submission. But the club that nations wield today can smash the planet.

The human race evolved over thousands of years through trial and error. During most of history, people could not foresee the consequences of their activities. They were in a state of dependence on natural forces beyond their control. With the development of human intellect, and particularly with acceptance of a scientific approach to the collection of knowledge, this situation changed. Although the forces of nature may escape forever total understanding and predictability, we have achieved the ability to foresee probable consequences and predict the likely outcome of many of the processes we use to change our environment.

The old trial-and-error method brought advances. People learned initially to make and use fire to help keep their environment more habitable. They learned to domesticate plants and animals and with these to support greater numbers of people in greater security. They learned to mine metals and minerals, to manufacture things, and to discover the energy sources that permitted the development of civilization and advanced technology. But the errors made were also great and sometimes caused the disappearance of those who took the wrong pathway or failed to understand the systems with which they were meddling. Damage to the environment was done many times in human experience. Local environmental crises have affected the welfare and existence of many peoples. But so long as human numbers were small and the world was large, so long as the diversity and strength of the natural world surrounded mankind and was not much diminished, most damage could be repaired. There was room and time for fresh starts and new directions.

Today we have lost the leeway for extensive trial and error in efforts to make environments of our own choosing. A wrong decision on the crops to be planted in China or India has threatened the survival of greater numbers of people than existed on all the earth a thousand years ago. A mistake in calculating the effect of supersonic planes on the upper atmosphere could conceivably imperil the existence of most life on earth. Failure to understand the consequences of atmospheric testing of hydrogen bombs has already brought risk to the health of all people.

The loss of any comfortable margin for error results not only from the enormous power available through new human technologies, and not only from the increase in people to numbers previously unbelievable. It results also from the decline in natural diversity, from the removal of the buffering and security offered by the presence over most of the planet of a wild world that had evolved through millions of years. With this decline and loss, the capacity of the biosphere to repair itself and to recuperate from the disruptions caused by man has been impaired seriously.

It is this precarious state of human affairs that makes it essential for all people to develop a better understanding of the ways in which the biosphere operates, and how the ecosystems that they may seek to modify are constructed and how they function. Ecology provides a means for such understanding. Although much is to be learned about life and environment, enough information is now available to provide a firmer base for human action than is currently being used. In this chapter a few of the ecological rules of the game are exampled. They are basic and one cannot afford to ignore them.

The Flow of Energy

For life to exist it must be supplied with energy. For the ecosystems of the earth the source of energy is sunlight. This is captured by green plants in the process called photosynthesis and used in combining simple, inorganic molecules of carbon dioxide from the air with water to form organic molecules, for example, simple sugars such as glucose. In this process a portion of the solar energy that strikes the plant surface is transformed into chemical energy stored within sugar molecules. This can then be used by the plant to synthesize the other compounds it requires to grow and reproduce. For this other chemicals must be obtained from the soil or from solution in water. These essential nutrients, such as nitrogen, calcium, magnesium, or potassium, along with sunlight, carbon dioxide and water, provide the raw materials from which all plant structures—from one celled algae to giant trees—are synthesized. They also provide the available food and energy for all animals and for those plants or microorganisms that lack the capacity for photosynthesis.

Photosynthesis is thus responsible for providing virtually all the food energy required by life on earth. It is the original source of most of man's food. Photosynthesis, carried out by plants in past ages, is responsible for the fossil-fuel energy stored in coal, petroleum, and natural gas, and is thus the source of most of the energy used by human societies.

During photosynthesis carbon dioxide is removed from the air, or from water in which it has dissolved, and oxygen is released. Virtually all of the existing oxygen in the atmosphere, on which all animal life depends, has been derived from photosynthesis in the past. This statement, however, requires some elaboration. Although plants produce oxygen during photosynthesis, they also consume oxygen during respiration. Like animals they must burn oxygen in order to carry out a wide variety of metabolic processes. Furthermore when plants die and their tissues decay oxygen is also consumed. Thus any single plant, from the day it first germinates to the day when it is totally decayed and returned to the soil both produces and consumes oxygen, and if the breakdown of its organic materials is complete after its death it will have made no net contribution of oxygen to the atmosphere. How then did the oxygen supply of the atmosphere accumulate? In fact, it represents the difference between the total amount of plant materials produced by photosynthesis in past ages, and those that have since been oxidized, broken down by the action of fire, decay processes, and the like. In other words, the oxygen of the air is balanced by the amount of reduced carbon represented by the undecomposed organic material still on earth.

During the 1960s concern was expressed that the rate of fossil-fuel consumption, oxidizing plant and animal materials produced in the past, could lead in time to a total depletion of the oxygen in the atmosphere. Even a significant decrease in the amount of oxygen could have serious consequences for many forms of life. However, an examination of this problem revealed no observable change in the percentage of oxygen in the air during the period for which measurements were available. Since this was a period of high consumption of fossil fuels, it appeared that the fears were unwarranted. Apparently the fossil fuels that we consume represent only a small proportion of the total organic material stored in rocks, soil, or other deposits. It is unlikely that we will run out of oxygen only from burning the concentrated deposits of fossil fuels that are recoverable under mining technologies. The other side of the coin, however, is the possibility of a marked increase in the carbon dioxide in the air, also resulting from the burning of fossil fuel. This is a more serious question, although perhaps less urgent than others that we now confront.

Food Chains and Productivity.   Energy stored by green plants becomes available to other organisms by being passed through *food chains,* which are simply a series of organisms that feed one on the other. Plant-eating animals, herbivores, obtain their food energy directly from green plants. Flesh-eating animals, carnivores, consume herbivores and receive food energy from plants second hand. Still other animals, supercarnivores, feed on other carnivores and are three or more links removed from the original energy source. In turn, parasites or decay organisms may obtain their energy from carnivores, herbivores, or directly from plants. Food chains are never long, since most of the energy present at any link is lost during the process of transfer from one link to another.

All natural communities, or ecosystems, are made up of organisms linked together through food chains. The chains are intertwined into intricate *food webs.* All are based on sunlight energy. This energy flows through ecosystems on the food chain pathway and is eventually lost to the ecosystem, although it may be stored for varying periods of time. For the ecosystem to keep functioning, continual new supplies of energy must be brought in via the sunlight-green plant interaction.

Similar links in different food chains are described as being at the same energy level, or *trophic level.* Thus all green plants form the *producer* trophic level. Herbivores occupy the second, *primary consumer* trophic level. Carnivores that feed on herbivores form the *secondary consumer* trophic level. Decay organisms form the *reducer* level, and so forth.

Since there is a necessary and unavoidable loss of energy in any transfer from one level to the next, it follows that a greater supply of food energy will be available, or be made available, at the producer level than at any level above it. More energy will be available in the herbivore level than in the carnivore level that feeds on it. With rooted plants, growing in soil, the total weight of organic material in the green plant level, its *biomass,* must be greater than the biomass represented by the bodies of herbivores. The herbivore biomass will in turn be larger than that of carnivores. This leads to the concept of *biotic pyramids,* which are diagrammatic ways of showing the relative biomass, number of organisms, or total energy storage in each of the trophic levels of a biotic community (Figs. 1, 2 and 3).

To understand the functioning of an ecosystem, however, a knowledge of the biomass involved is less important than a knowledge of the rate at which energy flows through the ecosystem. Energy flow through an ecosystem is a measure of its biological *productivity.* Productivity is the rate at which new organic material is produced in an ecosystem. It can be expressed in terms

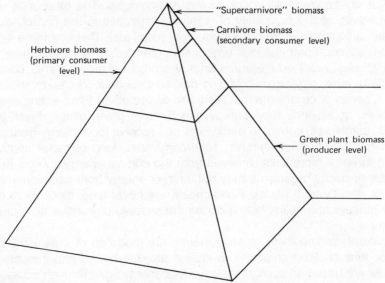

"Supercarnivore" biomass

Carnivore biomass
(secondary consumer level)

Herbivore biomass
(primary consumer
level)

Green plant biomass
(producer level)

figure 1
Theoretical pyramid of biomass, showing the weight of organisms supported at each
trophic level of a terrestrial food chain. Similar pyramids could illustrate the number
of organisms, or the calories of energy stored in each trophic level. In most natural
communities, however, the green plant biomass is proportionately much larger than
is shown here (see Figures 2 and 3).

of calories of energy fixed per unit of time, or more crudely in terms of increase
in biomass per unit of time, or in increase in numbers of organisms per unit
of time.

Productivity is a term with many meanings. It is commonly used to describe
efficiency of industrial processes, or to mean the amount of harvest or yield
from a farm or forest. But yield is at best an indirect measure of productivity,
since usually only a portion of what is produced, in the sense described here,
is removed in the form of yield or harvest.

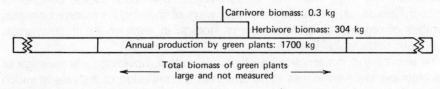

Carnivore biomass: 0.3 kg

Herbivore biomass: 304 kg

Annual production by green plants: 1700 kg

Total biomass of green plants
large and not measured

figure 2
Pyramid of biomass in an African thornbush area. Of the total herbivore biomass,
250 kg consist of herbivorous soil animals (mostly invertebrates). Data from
Hendrichs (1970) *Saugetierkund. Mitt. 18:* 237–255.

It is worth noting the difference between *gross* productivity, the rate at which energy is fixed by photosynthesis, and *net* productivity, the difference between energy fixed by photosynthesis and that lost through respiration. Furthermore, it is also worth noting that *primary* productivity refers to the fixing of solar energy by green plants, whereas *secondary* productivity is the production of new animal biomass by the consumers of green plants.

The Flow of Nutrients

The picture of an ecosystem presented thus far reveals it to be powered by solar energy that flows through green plants to food chains that are in turn tied in various food webs. However, these food chains and webs also serve in the flow of chemical nutrients. These nutrients may be derived from air, water, soil, or rock, but they are first synthesized by green plants into complex organic molecules—into carbohydrates, proteins, fats, oils, or other components of living creatures. These in turn are formed into the structures of which living cells are composed, and in complex organisms these are put together into tissues, organs, and organ systems.

Energy flows in one direction through an ecosystem, whereas mineral nutrients are cycled, meaning that they are reused again and again. Therefore, an ion of sulfur, obtained from the soil by grass roots, may come to rest in a plant protein molecule. This may be consumed by a deer and become a protein component of deer muscle. If the deer is eaten by a cougar the sulfur ion rests for a time in cougar muscle. Eventually the cougar dies and its body is consumed by reducer organisms. On the death of these the original sulfur ion will be returned to the soil from which it can enter a new food chain and go through another cycle. Essential nutrients, which are often in short supply in an ecosystem, can thus be kept in circulation and reused. They can be passed on from organism to organism over centuries or millenia.

It would be wrong to assume, however, that ecosystems are closed and that minerals cycle *ad infinitum*. Usually there is a movement of minerals into an ecosystem, carried by wind, water, or by mobile animals that move from one system to another such as migrating birds. Thus minerals picked up in its food supply by a golden plover wintering in the tropical Hawaiian Islands will be carried in its migration to the Alaskan arctic, and if the bird dies there will be incorporated into a tundra ecosystem. Minerals move out of ecosystems not only through animal movements but more directly through the various processes of soil erosion by wind or water. In a stable, undisturbed ecosystem, however, this flow of minerals is small in proportion to those minerals that remain in the system and are cycled within it. Disturbance of an ecosystem can result in a more rapid mineral drain, as through severe soil erosion, leading to its degradation. Continued degradation reduces its capacity to support life— bringing a decline in productivity.

Within the biosphere as a whole there is relatively little loss or gain of chemical materials. Everything remains to be recycled through one or another ecosystem, although some chemicals may be locked up for millions of years in deep rock deposits. Even these, however, may eventually reach the surface where they become exposed to the eroding action of wind and water and release their elements once more for use by the biosphere.

The rate of productivity in an ecosystem is commonly controlled by the availability and rate of cycling of essential nutrients. It is more usual for productivity to be slowed down by a shortage of some essential nutrient than by a shortage of solar energy—or at least this is true for ecosystems based on land. In the oceans, or deep lakes, absence of light is often critical.

Biological Magnification

Unfortunately for those who like to have all things simple and clearly defined, in the biosphere everything is tied to everything else in one way or another. In consequence, actions intended to accomplish only limited and planned-for effects may turn out to have other effects that are felt on the far side of the planet. People in general began to realize this after World War II when the United States and the Soviet Union started to put together atomic and then hydrogen bombs. The theory behind this exercise was that the nation that had the biggest, nastiest, or most of these instruments of terror could scare the other nation and the rest of the world into being good, and not interfering with the plans of the dominant nation. It didn't work out quite that way. Still, as part of this macabre game, the nation that developed a bigger or more vicious kind of bomb felt the necessity to test it, to see if it would work, and hopefully to scare the other nation. The little atomic bombs of World War II were enough to destroy two Japanese cities along with many of their people. But after the war bigger bombs were made and these also were to be tested. Obviously they could not be tested in inhabited areas where people who had votes or other power might object, so the American bombs were tested in remote Pacific islands—Bikini and Eniwetok—where the people were few and had no votes or political influence. The people were removed and the bombs set off. The local damage was enormous. But, that was only the beginning.

In the 1950s people learned about fallout. They learned that the air, which yesterday was the same old atmosphere that we had always lived with, could today become a lethal thing. It looked, smelled, and tasted the same, and didn't hurt a bit when it was breathed. But it was not the same. Invisible particles of stuff called radioactive isotopes, strontium 90, cesium 37, and others drifted down with the mist and rain, entered the soil and water, entered the grass and shrubs, entered the cows and sheep, and eventually into the human blood stream. Strontium 90 was a particular devil, since animal tissues tend to treat it similar to ordinary calcium and incorporate it in bone marrow and bone. From there the damaging radiation affects the cells of the surrounding tissues. One could not feel it, but if the radiation affected particular cells in particular ways cancer would develop, or perhaps damage to chromosomes would take place.

Scientists learned a great deal about the atmosphere in the 1950s and 1960s, following radioisotopes from where they were created, in the Pacific islands or the wild lands of Siberia, to where they finally came down and got into the milk and bread. They also learned much about the process of *biological magnification*. What appeared at first to be relatively harmless amounts of isotopes were concentrated along food chains until they were no longer harmless but deadly. People in general also learned a lot about political action. There were songs brought out by the pop singers: "What have they done to the rain?" or "Where have all the flowers gone?" There were Ban-the-Bomb marches. Scientists formed groups to refute the soothing words disseminated by the Atomic Energy Commission. Finally, the governments involved agreed to ban atmospheric testing. Unfortunately, other governments, notably France and China, did not get in on the earlier action. When they later developed their bombs they assumed the right to follow the same, stupid course. Hence, every now and then, another blast goes up into the stratosphere and over all the world the radiation counters start clicking madly. But experts tell us we're still OK (Commoner, 1967).

Biological magnification is not a new discovery. It was known that tunicates, or sea squirts, sea animals that represent a sort of evolutionary dead-end, along the line that gave rise to starfish, sand dollars, and their relatives, had the ability to concentrate vanadium. Vanadium is a rare element in sea water, yet tunicates living in the intertidal zone accumulate large quantities in their tissues. Why they should concentrate vanadium is not known, but they do. During the early decades of this century this information was not usually related to anything of human significance. Similarly it was known that the thyroids of mammals concentrate iodine, a rare element on land, although common enough in the marine environment where animals had evolved. Since iodine is essential for thyroid functioning, it was essential in an evolutionary sense for the thyroid gland to be able to hold on to any iodine that passed in the blood stream. But the atomic age brought with it quantities of iodine 134, a radioisotope that, when concentrated could destroy thyroid tissue and cause cancer.

Biological magnification is simple enough. Plants require various nutrients for growth and development, including such relatively rare elements as boron and zinc. Grass roots pick these up from wherever they find them in the soil, but once they are taken in they will be maintained in grass tissues. Some will become concentrated in the seeds so that the new plant, on germination, will have enough to get started. In the second stage, a white-footed mouse, for example, may feed on grass seeds. These seeds will contain more of element X than is to be found in any similarly sized sample of soil, air, or water. If element X is essential to the nutrition of the mice it may be used directly and held in the tissue or organ that requires it. If not it may be stored in fat for future use. However, having fed on thousands of grass seeds, the mouse is likely to contain more of element X than is to be found in any similar sized sample of the grass plants from which the seeds were obtained. Next along the line a red-tailed hawk may sweep over its hunting ground collecting mice whereever it can find them. And so it will acquire more of element X in this way. At any one time, hawk tissues will contain more X than mouse tissues and they in turn more than grass tissues.

An example of the degree of magnification is shown in studies carried out by Dr. Joseph Hickey and his associates (1966) in Lake Michigan. There the subject of study was not radioisotopes, but another man-made substance, DDT. The general environment, represented by bottom sediments from the lake contained 0.0085 parts per million of DDT. Small invertebrates, the microscopic floating animals or zooplankton of Lake Michigan, however, contained 0.041 parts per million. This is a concentration of 5 times over what was found in the environment from which they fed. Fish, which fed on zooplankton, contained from 3.00 to 8.00 parts per million, a concentration 100 times greater than was found in their food. The most spectacular jump, however, was found in the herring gulls that feed on fish. These contained an average of 3177 parts per million of DDT—400 times higher than in the fish on which they fed. A little multiplication shows that the concentration in herring gulls was from 200,000 to one million times higher than in the general aquatic environment. It is this degree of magnification that is frightening when the substance involved is a deadly radioisotope, or a poison such as certain pesticides.

Public concern over radioisotopes in the milk and meat was only reaching a peak when Rachel Carson in 1962 published her book *Silent Spring*. More than all of the scientific papers that preceded it, this alarm call aroused the public to consciousness of other invisible, tasteless, odorless components of their environment that were potentially as dangerous as strontium 90. These, the organic pesticides, were also a discovery that received impetus from World War II. In all previous wars insect-borne diseases had taken a heavy toll of soldiers and war refugees. In World War II this death and morbidity rate was much less. Credit was given to a "miracle" insecticide DDT, a chlorinated hydrocarbon synthesized in chemical laboratories and not occuring naturally in the biosphere. It meant death for insects, such as body lice, that carry typhus or the fleas that transmit bubonic plague. Following the war it was tried in malaria control and served to greatly reduce numbers of malaria mosquitoes and thus almost eliminate this disease from many tropical countries.

DDT was next used in agriculture and served to knock back crop-destroying insects. It was then taken up everywhere, used in most households in wealthy countries, used against garden pests, farm pests, and virtually anything thought likely to endanger human health or any crop in which people had an interest. During this time, however, other studies were going on and being quietly published in scientific journals. These reported massive damage to wildlife resulting from the use of DDT or its relatives. DDT was only one of a host of closely related chemicals and the least toxic of the lot. Others—aldrin, dieldrin, endrin, toxaphine, telodrin, heptachlor, the list is long—were more dangerous. Still others, not organochlorines, such as parathion, malathion, or TEPP, were often more toxic, but did not persist in the environment.

The new organochlorine pesticides were not, like many organic chemicals, appreciably broken down by metabolism in the organisms that happened to ingest them. They were not, in other words, highly biodegradable, but tended to retain their toxicity as they were passed along food chains and could do damage wherever they landed.

When Rachel Carson sounded the public alarm, our knowledge of the effects of organochlorines was minimal, but enough to cause concern. Subsequently the evidence began to accumulate. The virtual disappearance of many species of raptorial birds from the British Isles was related to the effect of organochlorines on their reproductive processes (Ratcliffe, 1967). Although the adults continued to live, with a heavy load of pesticide residues, they laid soft-shelled eggs, since the chemicals interfered with their calcium metabolism. The same effect was noted next in North America where virtually all species of raptors from kestrels to bald eagles were found to be affected to some degree by DDT. Next, various kinds of water birds, also high on their food chains, were found to be affected. The Bermuda petrel, the brown pelican, cormorants, murres, herons, and egrets were found to exhibit the soft-shelled phenomenon and to be declining in population. DDT concentration was then noted in fish, sea mammals, and in fact in most places where it was sought (Shea, 1969). Its effects on human health remained debatable, although some pointed out its capacity to act as a cancer-causing agent. Still more alarming were some studies that indicated it could have an effect on the productivity of phytoplankton (plant plankton), the floating green plants that form the base of marine food chains and support most of the world's aquatic life including its major fisheries. The full evidence against DDT remains to be discovered, but meanwhile efforts to ban it entirely or drastically reduce its use, along with the use of its more expensive relatives, have been partly successful in the technologically advanced countries. Unfortunately it is still being used in the developing countries where shortsightedness on the part of officials combines with the drastic need to produce more and more food for ever-expanding human populations.

Species Diversity

Although it is useful to regard ecosystems in the relatively simple terms employed thus far, to consider energy flow and mineral cycling and to sort out trophic, levels, food chains, webs, productivity and the like, it is essential to remember their full complexity and diversity. Even the simplest natural ecosystem is still too complex for our full understanding. The producer layer, for example, is not composed just of some uniform entity called green plants. In even a relatively small area it is composed of tens, or hundreds, or in the tropics perhaps thousands of species of plants. One small volcanic mountain in the Philippines supports more species of woody plants than are to be found in the entire United States. These species occur in recognizable plant communities, each characterized by a certain grouping of species, and these communities differ from place to place around the world. Each species plays a particular role in its community, and relates in different ways to other species in the community. Each has its own requirements within its habitat—its place in the total environment.

Feeding on the plants in any community will be a much greater number of species of animals. On land, insects are likely to make up the most numerous class, but in the ocean other invertebrates in the zooplankton will occupy the principal primary consumer roles. Usually less in number of species, but still great in variety will be the vertebrate animals—fish, reptiles, amphibians, birds, and mammals—that will occupy primary, secondary, or higher consumer levels (Figs. 3 and 4).

The place of any species in its environment, and the role that it plays within that place is known as the ecological niche of the species (Grinnell, 1928). It is said that each species occupies its particular ecological niche and that no two can occupy the same niche. It is said, further, that if two species with similar habitat requirements and playing similar environmental roles compete for the same niche, one will be displaced and will disappear from the community. It is difficult to prove this statement, since it is often difficult to see a niche if no species is occupying it, and it may sometimes appear that

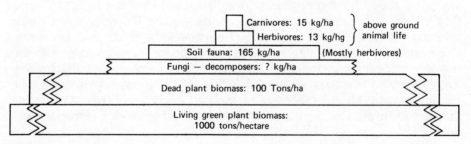

figure 3

Pyramid of biomass in an Amazonian rain forest. To show the consumer levels at all, the pyramid cannot be drawn to scale. 1,100,000 kg of living and dead green plant matter support 210 kg of animal consumers, a ratio of 5240 to 1. Data from Fittkau and Klinge (1973), *Biotropica* 5:2–14.

two species are actually carrying out the same sorts of activities within the same habitat. It has been noted that when one species is drastically reduced in numbers, another may move in and occupy, at least partially, its former niche. Thus the disappearance of the California sardine, once present in great numbers in the waters off the west coast of North America, allowed for a great increase in the anchovy, a fish occupying a similar place in the ecosystem. There is now debate as to whether the presence of anchovies is preventing the sardine from reoccupying its former niche. G. E. Hutchinson (1958) has attempted to clarify this problem by distinguishing between the fundamental niche of a species—the niche that it could occupy were other competing species not present, and the realized niche, the one actually occupied in the presence of predators, competitors, or other rivals.

In looking at any ecosystem, or at the biotic community that forms the functional part of the ecosystem, one is impressed by the larger or most conspicuous organisms. We call a particular community a forest because it is the dense stand of trees that is most obvious to the eye. But a forest ecosystem contains far more than trees. Another community will be called grassland since grasses are most conspicuous, but the entire ecosystem could be changed if various microorganisms were to disappear from the soil. These invisible components, such as the nitrogen-fixing bacteria, which take nitrogen from the atmosphere and transform it into the nitrates that grasses require, are essential to the community. The number of species of microorganisms living in the soil, on the soil surface, in the vegetation, or animal life may far exceed the number of species visible to the unaided eye. Each plays a role in the community. Each assists in some way in the functioning of the ecosystem. We know the importance of some species in some roles, such as the fungi that cause the breakdown of dead plant material. We do not know, and perhaps will never know, all of the niches and roles of species within a community. It is quite possible that some can be removed and the ecosystem will function as well as ever. It is also known that if some species are removed the ecosystem will change, begin to break down, or lose its productivity.

At one time mankind occupied a simple niche in a complex community and fitted in with its total functioning. But that day is past. Mankind has increased at the expense of much of the natural diversity of the planet. We have left behind the level of technology and human population that permitted the simple occupancy of a primate niche in a tropical community. Today the niche of technological mankind is global in extent and impinges on or destroys the niches of all other species.

Populations and Carrying Capacity

It is not possible to get far with the study of human impact on the environment without considering the growth and control of populations. A population, in an ecological sense, is the number of individuals of a species that occupy a particular area at a particular time. Like other phenomena in nature, populations are never static. They increase, decrease, and change composition from time to time. Populations are real enough, but among wild species they are seldom observed all at a time—exceptions being when colonial species cluster together in some open place, or those rare occasions when all individuals of a normally dispersed population happen to come out in the open. Usually populations are studied indirectly and statistically by sampling processes in which such characteristics as total numbers, density, sex and age structure, birth rate, and death rate, are examined. To determine the important characteristics of a population it is necessary to study it over a period of time—an easy enough process with short-lived microorganisms, but much more difficult with long-lived mammals or birds.

If a small population moves into a favorable environment not occupied by others of its species it will normally increase. For a time the birth or natality rate will exceed the death or mortality rate. If there is no further movement into or out of the area the population size at any time will be controlled by the balance between natality and mortality. Any environment, however, has limits. These limits may be imposed by the presence of suitable food plants, by the distribution of water in relation to food, by the availability of shelter against the elements, or the presence of suitable breeding areas, nesting sites, denning sites, and the like. As populations grow in any area they will begin to approach the limits where they can be supported. As they do so, more and more individuals find difficulty in obtaining the necessities of life. They will, in consequence, weaken and die. As the environmental limits are approached, therefore, the mortality will increase, whereas natality is likely to decline.

A point will be reached where natality equals mortality and at that point the population could stabilize and remain at a constant level. Most often such an ideal balance does not occur. Instead a population may temporarily overshoot the limits of its environment and then die off in large numbers, only to recover in time when births again exceed deaths. Some kinds of animals will damage their environment, and reduce its capacity by killing off the more nutritious food plants. If this occurs there may be a die-off not followed by recovery, or recovery only to a lower level determined by the reduced food supply.

The capacity of a population to increase under the most favorable conditions is determined by the maximum numbers of young that may be produced by the breeding individuals per unit of time, the percentage of breeding individuals in the total population, and the longevity of its members. A population exhibiting its maximum potential rate of increase is said to be increasing at its *biotic potential rate*. This occurs only when environmental factors are most favorable, when mortality is at a minimum and natality is at a maximum. Usually unfavorable factors in the environment prevent this biotic potential from being expressed. The sum of these unfavorable factors, which lead to increased deaths or decreased births, are referred to as the *environmental resistance*. Environmental resistance increases as a population begins to approach the limits of its environment (Figs. 5 and 6).

Those factors that together make up the environmental resistance are known as *limiting factors*. A limiting factor is a condition in the environment that approaches or exceeds the limits of tolerance of an individual, population, or larger group (Odum, 1971). It may be an essential nutrient that is in short supply, weather that is too hot or too cold to allow a particular species to thrive, the shortage of water, or the presence of other species that compete with or prey on the population being considered.

The capacity of an area to support a population of any species is known as its *carrying capacity* and is defined in terms of the number of individuals of a species that can be supported at any given time (Fig. 6). The growth of any population is limited by the carrying capacity of the environment in the area under consideration. Carrying capacity thus represents a level around which a population may stabilize and remain relatively constant. More often it represents a level around which population numbers tend to fluctuate, being sometimes higher but more often lower. However, above the level determined

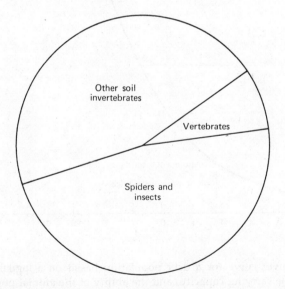

figure 4
Composition of animal biomass in an Amazonian rain forest. Most of the biomass is found in or on the soil and is likely to be overlooked by the nonspecialist. Soil fauna in this area consists of 929 million individual animals per hectare. Data from Fittkau and Klinge (1973), *Biotropica* 5:2–14.

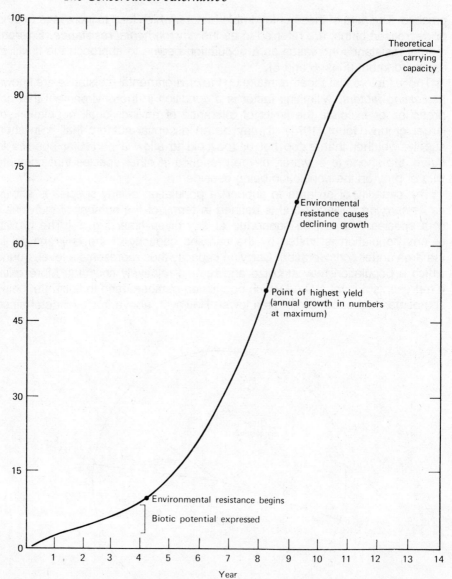

figure 5
Theoretical growth curve for a deer population based on a logistic formula. This assumes a stable carrying capacity, and the ability of the animal population to level off when carrying capacity is reached—two conditions that are not usually found in natural communities (from Dasmann, 1964, *Wildlife Biology*).

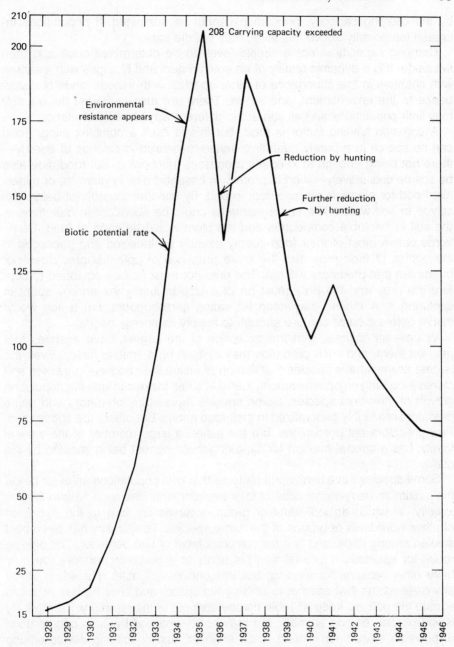

figure 6
Actual curve of population growth and decline in the George Reserve Deer Herd, Michigan (from Dasmann, 1964, *Wildlife Biology*).

by the carrying capacity, population cannot be sustained. If populations increase temporarily above this level, they will die back.

Carrying capacity is not a simple level, to be determined once and then set aside. It is a dynamic quality of an environment and changes with weather, with changes in the abundance of other species, with various kinds of disturbance to the environment, and so on. There are many different factors that may limit populations and all can act in different ways at different times.

A common limiting factor is food, but this is itself a complex thing. Food can be scarce in a purely quantitive sense measured in calories of energy—there not being enough to keep life processes functioning. But food may also be scarce qualitatively—short in protein, in essential oils, in vitamins, or minerals. Food for plants is represented, in part, by minerals capable of being dissolved in soil water. The same elements could be abundant in quantities in the soil in insoluble compounds and the plant would be short of food. Carnivores obtain most of their food supply already synthesized and packaged in the bodies of their prey. But the mere presence of potential prey does not guarantee that predators will eat. The predator must first be equipped to capture the prey and the prey must be of a size to justify the energy spent in capturing it. A mouse may keep fat eating grasshoppers, but a lion would starve before it could capture enough to supply its energy needs.

Virtually all animals, with the exception of the largest, have enemies that prey on them, and such predation may in itself be a limiting factor. Even the largest animals have species that live on or inside their bodies—parasites and disease-causing organisms among them. At times these can limit the population growth of their host species. Some species have many predators and some predators are highly generalized in their food habits. But others are specialized. Few predators eat porcupines, but the fisher, a large member of the weasel family, has a special method for capturing them without being impaled by the quills.

Some species have behavioral patterns that limit populations at levels below the maximum carrying capacity of their environment. One such pattern is *territoriality,* in which an individual or group occupies an area to the exclusion of other individuals or groups of the same species. Territoriality has been best studied among birds, and is a conspicuous facet of bird behavior. The singing robin, for example, is proclaiming his rights to a particular territory (he may have other reasons for singing, but this one is verifiable). He will drive off any male robins that attempt to occupy his space, and after he has acquired a mate the pair will keep all robin competitors out of their territory. Territoriality is widespread among animals, but may not be marked by such conspicuous displays as those seen among birds. A similar kind of spacing device among plants involves the production of metabolic substances that act as antibiotics in the soil, or inhibit the germination of seeds, or the growth of seedlings in the vicinity of the established adult plant.

A number of different forms of population limitation can operate on a species population over a period of years. Territoriality may normally restrict a population, but in some years the presence of many predators could hold the populations below the levels that the territories could support. In other years food supply could be reduced by weather and the normal territorially determined limits could not be supported. An unseasonable storm may destroy food and cover and drastically reduce a population. All of these factors can change the carrying capacity of a habitat from year to year.

Within any population, furthermore, there is a wide range of genetic variation. Some individuals are better adapted to resist droughts than others, some are more adept at escaping predators, some can tolerate higher levels of toxic chemicals in their diets, and so on. Thus the population is equipped to survive, through the survival of the best adapted individuals, to the spectrum of changes that can be expected to occur within its environment over long periods of time, and may have the genetic capacity to survive changes that exceed the normal range of expectable variation.

Into these exceedingly complex natural conditions mankind introduces simplistic, problem-solving methods. One of these is population control by use of broad-spectrum, persistent pesticides. DDT may be toxic to most members of an insect population, or perhaps even to all of them if the level is high enough and all of them can be reached. But it is most likely that some members of any pest population will be more resistant to DDT. Thus DDT can change the genetic makeup of a pest population to create a DDT-resistant race of insects. This has happened, notably with certain cotton pests, and it has been found in some places that these insects can become resistant, not only to DDT, but to virtually all of the other pesticides as well. Thus man creates "superpests."

Since DDT and its relatives affect not only the target insects but also most other forms of life as well, they destroy normal biological controls. Thus, if a species is normally kept within bounds by predation from other insects, spiders, mites, or birds, and DDT reduces or eliminates these enemies, the results are predictable. The more resistant pests, or the escapees, can, without natural checks, build up faster to higher levels than ever before. A minor infestation becomes a major plague. Furthermore, by destroying natural predators, other insects that were not previously pests may be able to increase sufficiently to become serious problems. Thus the pesticide creates new pests. All of these effects are now well known and have been demonstrated in many areas (Conway, 1965; Farvar and Milton, 1972). But certain pesticides are cheap, relatively easy to use, and do control pests in some areas, for a time. Their use continues, particularly where ignorance prevails. In some circumstances, and they are few, the use of even the most environmentally dangerous pesticide can be justified, providing the use is carefully controlled and the operators are fully aware of the dangers. But these are special circumstances.

Although mankind has grown adept at postponing payment on environmental debts, human populations must necessarily operate under the same basic rules that affect other animal, or plant, populations. Population levels are determined by the balance of births and deaths, influenced by the movement into (immigration) or out of (emigration) the area involved. An area at any time will have a carrying capacity for people, although this may be more variable and subject to influence than the carrying capacities of natural areas for wild species.

Mankind, through advances in technology, has greatly increased the carrying capacities of many of the areas occupied by people, and in some places can increase them still farther. But ultimate limits remain beyond which no conceivable advances in technology can raise carrying capacities. Most hopefully, humanity is capable, through socially induced behavior, of regulating human numbers. Human populations can be stabilized at levels well below the maximum that could be supported, thus providing relative abundance for all. It is this latter human capacity, as yet not widely demonstrated, that holds most hope for the future.

In considering the implications of the material considered thus far, it is necessary to note that the individual, whether human, animal, or plant, *does not and cannot* exist apart from its environment. Individuals exist only as a focus for the flow of energy and materials through space and time. They are always a part of a greater whole—the ecosystem, biosphere, or beyond that, the universe. Yet, at the same time, the individual through living and playing its role affects in some way the population, the biotic community, the ecosystem, and the biosphere, and thus to some degree, the universe. The full implications of this situation—ecological and philosophical—have yet to be appreciated.

References

Carson, Rachel, 1962. *Silent spring*. Houghton Mifflin, Boston.

Commoner, Barry, 1967. *Science and survival*. Viking, New York.

Conway, R. G., 1965. Crop pest control and resource conservation in tropical Southeast Asia. *Conservation in tropical Southeast Asia*. IUCN Publishing, New Series, 10: 159–163.

Dasmann, R. F., 1964. *Wildlife biology*. John Wiley, New York.

Elton, Charles, 1927. *Animal ecology*. Macmillan, New York (3rd Ed., 1947).

Farvar, M. Taghi and J. P. Milton, eds., 1972. *The careless technology*. Doubleday/Natural History Press, New York .

Grinnell, Joseph, 1928. The presence and absence of animals. University of California Chronicles, 30: 429–450.

Hickey, Joseph J., J. A. Keith, and F. B. Coon, 1966. An exploration of pesticides in a Lake Michigan ecosystem. *Journal of Applied Ecology, 3* (suppl.): 141–154.

Hutchinson, G. Evelyn, 1958. Concluding remarks, Cold Springs Harbor Symposium. *Quantitative biology, 22*:415–427.

Krebs, Charles J., 1972. *Ecology. The experimental analysis of distribution and abundance.* Harper and Row, New York.

Leopold, Aldo, 1933. *Game management.* Scribner's, New York.

Odum, Eugene P., 1971. *Fundamentals of ecology.* W. B. Saunders, Philadelphia, 3rd ed.

Ratcliffe, Derek, 1967. Decrease in eggshell weights in certain birds of prey. *Nature, 215*:208–210.

Shea, Kevin P., 1969. Unwanted harvest. *Environment, 11*: 12–16, 28–31.

Watts, Alan, 1969. The book on the taboo against knowing who you are. Abacus ed., 1973. Sphere Books, London, p. 16.

chapter three

Not Enough for too Many

"Oh daddy won't you take me back to Muehlenberg County.
Down by the green river where Paradise lay?
I'm sorry my son, but you're too late in asking.
Mr. Peabody's coal train has hauled it away."

John Prine, "Paradise"

Energy

Petroleum and the Energy Crisis

The year 1973 was most unusual. Through a strange combination of circumstances the people of the urban-industrial world realized for the first time the message that conservationists had been preaching for decades—that there are limits to the earth, and that sooner or later essential resources will run out. Naturally enough, some of them blamed the conservationists for the situation that had been predicted.

It began with another flare-up in the quarter-century old, useless war between Arabs and Israelis. This time the Arabs had hoped to steal a march

39

by attacking while the Israelis were sitting down to dinner in honor of their religious holiday, Yom Kippur. It did not quite work out. The Israelis dropped their table napkins, jumped into their tanks and jets, and the killing went on much as before. However, the Arabs were determined to teach a lesson to those nations that too fervently supported the Israeli cause—notably the United States and the Netherlands, and by way of warning, Western Europe and Japan. The oil-producing Arab states either cut off, or sharply reduced the supply of petroleum to the industrialized world. Suddenly the oil from Saudi Arabia, Kuwait, Abu Dhabi and other producing countries ceased to come through in its usual flow. The industrialized world panicked. Stock markets, currencies, and governments had been caught unprepared, despite repeated earlier warnings.

The message that the Arab states had hoped to transmit was "back down, take our side, give us a fair deal." The message that came through was "the end of petroleum resources really is in sight. We can no longer depend on our usual sources of supply and must seek alternatives to an oil-dependent technology." The "energy crisis" had arrived.

Paradoxically, there was no immediate energy shortage—not during 1973 or 1974. There was still oil, coal, and other fossil fuel in the ground. Nuclear power was being developed. In some countries hydropower was in good supply. Other sources of energy were being explored, but with an apparent abundance of cheap petroleum there had been no serious effort toward their development. However, the political maneuver of the oil-rich states combined with a lack of foresight and planning by governments of the industrialized world to produce a serious problem. For the average American, almost totally dependent on his eight-cylinder, gasoline-guzzling, mechanical monster to get to and from work or the grocery store the crisis was real enough. That there was still enough petroleum underground in the United States for current needs was a fact best known to the oil companies.

The worldwide effects of the petroleum cutback were instructive. The U.S.-S.R. and its eastern European allies were in good shape with more than enough fossil fuel for decades to come, and little interest in Arab oil. China, still scarcely industrialized, had a surplus of oil. Western Europe, however, had no internal sources of oil and had neglected the full development of its relatively abundant coal reserves. Production from the oil-rich strata under the North Sea was still only a future prospect. Japan had no alternative fuel sources. The last time its oil supply had been threatened, before World War II, it had struck out and captured a large share of the world in its reaction. This time it was nonviolent, but its economy showed signs of impending collapse. Hardest hit of all were the supporters of the Arabs, the developing nations, that had scarcely been able to afford oil at the old, low prices, and now saw their development plans falling apart. Most serious was the threat to food supplies, geared increasingly to the Green Revolution with its dependence on oil-powered agricultural machinery, and fertilizers produced from or by petroleum and natural gas.

Certainly the effects of the action by the oil-exporting nations exceeded the expectations of those who decided to put pressure on the industrialized world. The long-term effects can scarcely be predicted in 1974. One cannot know if the governments and peoples of the industrialized nations will learn the obvious lesson, that the old ways of living cannot continue. In mid-1974 it appears that they will not, that they must first be hit still harder.

Difficulties are encountered if one attempts to look at the availability of petroleum and the probable length of time that the supply will last. One lies in the confusing terminology. Thus petroleum reserves are not "reserves" in the usual sense of that word. Instead they are defined in relation to economics and technology. Thus the statement that there are one billion barrels of oil reserves somewhere does not mean that there are only one billion barrels of oil left in that location. It does mean that there are one billion barrels that the oil industry is willing to pump to the surface and sell under current prices and with existing costs of production. If the price of petroleum doubles and costs remain the same, reserves may "miraculously" increase.

A second term used by the oil industry is "resources." However, this is also defined in terms of economics and technology. If at *x* future date the oil-pumping technology has improved to *y* level, and costs and prices are at *z* level, then the oil resources can be calculated. The question "how much oil is there really?" refers to a third term that is used by the industry, the "resource base." This is the actual sum total of petroleum believed to exist in a particular location (Whittemore, 1973). Unfortunately, for our curiosity, we find that the petroleum industry is hesitant about telling us what the reserves are, what the resources are, or what is the resource base. In the United States the government is largely dependent on the industry for this information, and does not have independent means for determining it. The industry, made up of various companies in competition with one another, is not required to reveal facts that might undermine the competitive position of one company or another. Thus the public is not left entirely in the dark, since government estimates of petroleum reserves and resources base are available, but they are left with inadequate information.

Fortunately we do not need exact data on the full extent of the petroleum resource base to make a reasonable estimate on how long our oil supply will last. For example, Meadows and associates at the Massachusetts Institute of Technology have built mathematical models for use in forecasting the future of resources, population, technology, and of the like, which takes into account past trends, and likely future trends in rates of growth and rates of consumption. Their results, published in 1972 in *The Limits to Growth,* have stirred up controversy among model makers, economists, and futurologists. Nevertheless, the global picture presented in *The Limits to Growth* reveals prospects for the future that are not encouraging, and that have led to a general recognition of the need to reverse many existing trends. To determine the future prospects for petroleum, Meadows et al. assume an available world supply of 455 billion barrels, based on 1970 data from the U. S. Bureau of Mines. Assuming no increase in present rates of consumption, this supply would be exhausted in 31 years (by 2001 A.D.). However, rates of consumption have been increasing and are expected to continue to increase. Taking this into account, the petroleum supply would be essentially exhausted in 20 years, or by 1990 A.D. Since, as we have seen, estimates of available petroleum are unreliable, Meadows, et al. make a further prediction based on the assumption that there is five times more petroleum than the current estimates would indicate. If this were true, and assuming a continuing increase in rates of consumption, the world's petroleum would be largely used up in 50 years, or by 2020 A.D.

No matter how we juggle these figures, the picture remains dismal for economies that have learned to rely on petroleum for transportation, industry, electric power, and a great variety of manufactured products such as various plastics, medicines, and agricultural fertilizers. Between 1990 and 2020 the petroleum will be gone if we continue to use it as we have in the past. We have safely only 20 years to find alternative sources of fuel for most of the purposes for which we use petroleum today. If we are wise we will use it only for those purposes for which no effective substitutes can be found, and we will switch to alternative fuels as quickly as possible.

Since one may argue with the calculations used in *The Limits to Growth,* other estimates should be examined. Economist Eugene Ayres (1956) estimated that United States petroleum production would peak in 1970 and thereafter decline, whereas world petroleum production would peak in 2000 A.D. and then decline. Hans Landsberg (1964) wrote that United States petroleum would last until 1980 and that thereafter we would have to rely on foreign sources. Preston Cloud and M. King Hubbert, geologists, reported in 1969 that world petroleum production would peak between 1990 and 2000 and then rapidly decline (Cloud, 1969). One of the most optimistic estimates is by L.G. Weeks, who believed that the amount of petroleum ultimately recoverable from all land and offshore sources amounted to 2200 billion barrels. This is slightly less than the outside estimate of Meadows, et al.—2275 billion barrels.

The United States, with only six percent of the world's people, consumes one third of the petroleum produced in the world each year. However, in 1973 most of the petroleum consumed in the United States was produced at home. Hence the Arab oil boycott had only a marginal impact on the United States economy. By contrast, Western Europe imported all of its oil and mostly from Arab sources. Of the oil used in the United States, 53 percent is used for transportation. By contrast only 23.1 percent of the oil used in Europe is used for transportation. In the United States, road transportation—private motor cars, trucks, and buses—consumes 43.5 percent of the total petroleum used. In

Europe the figure is 17.6 percent (Leach, 1973). The way out is obvious. Other sources of fuel must be found, and soon, to run America's vehicles. Furthermore, the United States must anticipate a time when it will receive far less than one third of the world's petroleum supply.

Energy Resources (Nonnuclear)

It is necessary to look far beyond petroleum if we are to make any estimate of the energy future of the human race. If we do this we will find that the prospects for supplying energy to meet reasonable needs for civilization are encouraging, providing that we do not expect to cater to an ever-increasing energy demand (Fig. 7). The following brief review is introductory, and the prospects for these various energy resources will be discussed later.

Renewable Energy

1. *Solar energy.* Sunlight is the source of most other forms of energy on earth, with the exception of nuclear energy, tidal energy, and geothermal energy. It represents an enormous daily supply of energy reaching the earth from the sun (Table 1), and a supply that is, in human terms, inexhaustible. Although people use solar energy indirectly, in a variety of forms to be described below, and directly, if inefficiently in space heating and in maintaining body temperatures, for the most part solar energy is wasted. It could be used directly and efficiently to reduce or eliminate the need for any other type of fuel in the heating of buildings. It also can be used for the generation of electricity.

2. *Vegetational energy.* This is energy directly derived from solar energy through the process of photosynthesis. It has been used by people directly, in the form of plant foods, and indirectly in the form of animal foods, since humanity first appeared on earth. As food energy it is the one *essential* source of energy for the human race. Over most of the time that mankind was evolving, it was the only source of energy. Energy from vegetation, or animal products derived from it, is also used as fuel. Wood fuel, organic wastes such as animal dung, and other kinds of vegetation and animal products provide most of the energy used (apart from food calories) by most people in the developing nations of the world. Since humanity first learned the use of fire, organic fuels have been important for survival, particularly as people ventured from the tropics into cold climates. By making a wider range of foods palatable, these forms of energy also have increased the amount of food energy available to mankind. Despite the long history of use, however, we have yet to develop efficient and sustainable techniques to make large-scale use of vegetational energy. Its potential contribution to human needs is thus abused or neglected.

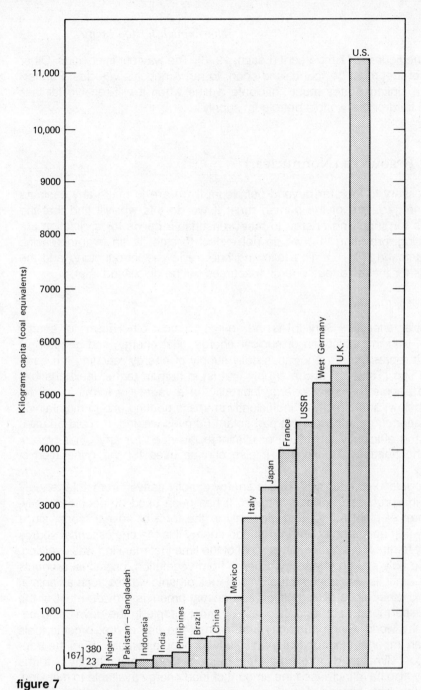

figure 7

Per capita energy consumption in 1971 in the 15 most populous nations. Figures include coal, lignite, petroleum, natural gas, hydropower, and nuclear power. Data from Brown, Lester R., 1974. *In the human interest.* W. W. Norton, New York, 190 pp. p. 32.

table 1

Estimated Potential Energy Resources of the Earth [a] (All Figures Expressed in Thousands of Terawatt Hours [b])

Energy Sources	Continuously Renewed Yearly Supply	Nonrenewable Energy Stores
Solar Energy		
Solar radiation	350,000	
Solar energy stored for brief periods		
Wood, waste	50	
Waterpower, potential	30	
developed	3	
Wind power	200	
Sea thermal power	100	
Tidal Power	1	
Geothermal Energy, available minimum	10	
Fossil Fuels		
Coal, known and accessible		6000
Oil, known and accessible		1000
Natural gas, known and accessible		400
Tar sands (Canada)		200
Oil shales (USA), not necessarily accessible		1500
Nuclear Fuels		
Uranium 235 for conventional reactors		1500
Uranium-thorium for breeder reactors		100,000,000
Tritium-Deuterium for theoretical fusion reactors		300,000,000,000

Note Total world energy consumption in 1970 was 50 thousand terawatt hours, equal to the amount shown as continually supplied by wood wastes.

[a] Adapted from Lars Kristoferson, 1974 (*Ambio,* 2: 181) and A. Lovins (1973)

[b] A terawatt equals 10^{12} watts and is a measure of the total thermal energy content of the various sources.

3. *Water energy.*   Power derived from moving water also originates in solar energy, since it is through sunlight that water is evaporated from the oceans, carried through the atmosphere, and ultimately deposited in the form of precipitation in rivers, streams, and other inland water bodies. Water power or hydropower has been used since the early days of civilization to turn simple water wheels that in turn were used for milling grain, pumping water for irrigation, or other purposes. Water energy also has been used to provide transportation along streams and rivers or in ocean currents. Like vegetational energy, hydropower is renewable and inexhaustible if properly managed. Although it is now developed locally to contribute an important supply of electricity in areas suitable to the construction of hydroelectric dams, its full potential has yet to be realized, and its total present contribution to the energy budget of civilization is small.

4. *Wind energy.*   Power derived from moving air also originates in solar energy, since it is the differential heating of the atmosphere by sunlight that determines the global circulation of the air. From the early days of civilization wind power has been used to turn windmills that in turn provided for the pumping of water, the grinding of grain, and other kinds of work. Until the present century, wind power moved most of the world's ocean transportation in the form of sailing ships. Although efficient wind generators exist through which wind power can be used to produce electricity, the development of this form of energy has been generally neglected in modern civilization. It represents an enormous energy resource, however, and one that is inexhaustible.

5. *Tidal energy.*   Energy present in the oceans' tidal movements derives from the combined gravitational pull of the moon and the sun on the waters of the earth. Although not appreciably developed anywhere as yet, it represents another potential and inexhaustible energy resource for coastal communities.

6. *Ocean thermal gradient energy.*   Particularly in tropical seas there is a marked temperature difference between surface waters and deep waters. It has been calculated that this could be used to develop electric power, however the technology for doing so has yet to be developed.

7. *Geothermal energy.*   This is energy available from hot springs, geysers, volcanoes, or potentially from any area of the earth's crust where a strong temperature gradient exists between the surface and underlying rocks. Hot springs and geysers have been developed locally to supply important amounts of electrical power. For the most part, however, this energy source has been neglected or ignored. Potentially it could represent an inexhaustible, large energy resource.

The relative availability of energy from each of the above sources, as compared with energy available from fossil fuels or from nuclear sources is shown in Table 1. However, with the exception of hydropower, and locally the use of wood and other organic fuels, these energy resources have been neglected in favor of fossil fuels and nuclear power. These two remaining energy sources, therefore, will be discussed at greater length, before we consider the prospects for a more balanced energy development. However, for most of human existence, until the last century, people existed without any dependence on fossil fuel and with no knowledge of nuclear power. The dependence on fossil fuels, and the problems associated with both fossil fuel and nuclear energy, are a peculiar feature of the present urban-industrial culture, and a reflection of its apparent incapacity to recognize either ultimate limits of obvious side effects.

Fossil Fuels. Fossil fuels result from the interactions between sunlight and vegetation during periods in the earth's history when conditions were favorable for abundant growth, but only limited decomposition of living things. Fossil fuels are essentially nonrenewable under present conditions. Over a period of millions of years of abundant plant growth, they could be renewed. But in terms of human life spans and our ability to look into the future we must consider that the present fossil fuel resource is all that we are likely to have.

Coal. Coal was the first fossil fuel to be used extensively by civilization and is still the most abundant. It can be converted into petroleum or into the various raw materials for industry now derived from petroleum, but only with an expenditure or energy, and at an economic cost that was discouraging for as long as oil was cheap. According to Meadows, et al. the known supplies of coal are sufficient to last 2300 years under present rates of use. However, with the expected expansion of energy use, and the exhaustion of petroleum resources, the known supplies of coal would run out in 111 years. If this expansion took place and reserves were five times as great as are presently believed, the supply would last 150 years.

Coal is difficult to obtain from deep mines, and there is a serious risk to human life involved. Surface or strip mines are environmentally destructive. Great areas of land, 4 million acres in the United States have already been devastated by surface mining. Strip mining for coal is responsible for 41 percent of this damage. Furthermore, coal is difficult to transport, compared to oil, and it has not been economically competitive with oil during the past century. This condition is now changing.

Petroleum. The situation in relation to this fuel has been reviewed.

Natural Gas. Natural gas, resulting from the decomposition of organic materials, is commonly found in association with petroleum, but may occur in separate deposits, or in association with coal fields. Its supply, rate of consumption, and probable future are comparable to that of petroleum, and the available life of known or predictable resources is not any greater (Meadows, et al., 1972). It is a valued fuel at the present time because it is clean, nonpolluting, and particularly useful in the production of nitrogen fertilizers.

Tar Sands. These are known principally from Alberta, Canada, and represent a low-grade source of petroleum not usually considered in calculating petroleum reserves. Under past conditions of low-cost oil it was not economically feasible to derive petroleum from tar sands. Now it is considered to be profitable to do so. However, there is serious question as to whether the total expenditure of energy required to extract petroleum from tar sands will be less than the energy obtained from the oil thus obtained. It is likely that only a small percentage of the tar sands will prove to be productive of energy. In any event the total known availability of petroleum from tar sands does not equal more than one fifth of the known petroleum reserves. This resource will serve, therefore, only to string out the petroleum reserves for a few years longer (Lovins, 1973).

Oil Shales. In theory, oil shales are a major source of future petroleum. It has been estimated that 16,500 square miles of Colorado, Utah, and Wyoming are covered with oil shales that contain from 600 billion to 3000 billion barrels of oil. This is more than the estimated total world petroleum reserve (Sterba, 1974). In fact, there is serious doubt that this amount would be recoverable. Oil shales consist of a hydrocarbon called kerogen contained in rocks known as marlstone. When these rocks are heated to 900 degrees the kerogen is converted into shale oil, which is equivalent to petroleum. However, one is left with an expanded amount of rock debris to be disposed of. The industrial process requires great amounts of water, which is in scarce supply in the regions where the oil shales occur. The energy budget of oil shale mining requires critical study (Odum, 1973). There are reasons to believe that the total energy input into the process will exceed the energy output. Of course, if part of the input is provided by public subsidy, for example, in road construction, services to towns, and processing plants, or more directly—then it would still be "profitable" for the exploiter to develop the oil shale resources. The public, in addition to paying part of the bill, would receive a negative energy return. The environmental damage caused by oil shale development, particularly in the dry intermountain region of the west, would be enormous. There would be little hope of revegetating mined land or the spoil banks, since water would not be available. Under these circumstances one can only wonder in 1974 about the apparent willingness of the federal government to encourage the exploitation of oil shale resources. One would be justified in questioning whether the government was working for the people or for the exploiters.

This review of the fossil-fuel future leaves the writer in little doubt that by the end of this century, unless patterns of consumption change, we can expect petroleum and natural gas to be available in small quantities and at high cost. Thereafter, urban-industrial civilization, if it were to continue along its present course, would have to rely on coal, with some supplements from oil shale and tar sands, to meet the demands for fuels and other raw materials that have been supplied in recent decades from petroleum.

There is, however, one further fossil-fuel resource that requires special mention. This is peat. Peat can be described as vegetation halfway on the road to becoming coal. It is found particularly in cold, acid bogs in arctic and subarctic climates. The cutting and removal of peat on any large scale can involve massive destruction of wild natural areas in the northern hemisphere. At best, the availability of peat will string out the lifetime of other fossil-fuel resources by a few decades if we do not assume a reversal of present trends. However, under more reasonable conditions of demand, peat could be used to supply local energy needs in many northern countries. It already supplies an appreciable amount of the fuel needs in Ireland.

Nuclear Energy

It has been said by its proponents that the discovery of nuclear energy came just in time to save civilization from a slow death following the exhaustion of its supplies of fossil fuel (McPhee, 1973). Others might question, in view of the damage already caused, whether the slow death of a fossil-fuel technology might not be preferable to the destruction of Hiroshima and Nagasaki, let alone the constant threat of nuclear annihilation under which humanity continues to live. Nevertheless, nuclear power is here, and in any forecast of the future must be figured in.

Nuclear technology is perhaps the most complicated known to man. In consequence, the average citizen is in the dark about what is going on, and is forced to rely on the knowledge and skills of a variety of technical experts. Since these experts often disagree, most people are left with a feeling of suspicion and no small amount of fear concerning the whole process. Although one group of experts assures them that a nuclear power plant cannot explode like an atom bomb, another group will point out that in the event of a, not unlikely, breakdown human life could be seriously endangered throughout an extensive area. In fact, accidents have occurred repeatedly in existing nuclear power plants, and on many occasions safety systems have failed to operate. Although a nuclear plant may not explode like an atom bomb, it can in the event of certain types of breakdown allow the escape of great quantities of radioactive materials into the surrounding environment that would endanger human life perhaps for distances of a hundred miles or more from the plant. That no such escape has taken place as yet is in part a matter of luck, and in part the willingness of power-plant workers to risk their lives while trying to repair malfunctioning systems (Stockholm Conf. Eco, 1972).

Nuclear Fission. Nuclear power at the present time is derived from the naturally radioactive metal uranium. Uranium in nature occurs in two forms that are mixed together, uranium 235, which is used in nuclear fission plants, and uranium 238, which cannot be used except after treatment. Uranium 235 has a nucleus that splits spontaneously into smaller fragments releasing neutrons and great amounts of energy. One pound of uranium 235, subject to complete fission, as in an atomic explosion, can give off as much energy as 1500 tons of coal. Unfortunately, uranium 235 is relatively scarce in nature and must be separated from uranium 238 by an elaborate process (CEQ, 1973). The process commonly used is gaseous diffusion. In this the original uranium oxide, mined from the ground is chemically changed into another compound, uranium hexafluoride, which in turn is readily changed into a gaseous state. Since molecules of the uranium 235 hexafluoride are lighter, it is possible by allowing them to diffuse through a porous wall to build up a higher concentration of uranium 235 on one side of the wall. This more concentrated uranium 235 is converted into uranium dioxide that is then used as the fuel in the nuclear power plant (Lovins, 1973; McPhee, 1973).

Gaseous diffusion plants are enormous installations. The one at Oak Ridge, Tennessee, built during World War II is the size of a small city and took two years to build. Unfortunately for the energy balance it runs on electricity produced at this time by the Tennessee Valley Authority from hydroelectric power plants, and from coal-fired plants fueled with coal that has been strip mined from the surrounding area. It has been estimated that when this plant was running full blast during World War II it alone used one sixth of the nation's total electrical power output. In 1967 there were three gaseous diffusion plants in operation, and together they used 4 percent of the nation's electrical power. In 1972 the output of all existing nuclear power plants contributed no more than 2 percent of the nation's electrical power. Thus the nuclear plants did not generate enough to power their own diffusion systems. It should also be noted that great quantities of fossil fuel are used in mining uranium ore, transporting it to the diffusion plants, transporting the enriched fuel to the power plants, and then transporting, processing, and storing radioactive wastes from the plants. The total energy budget of the system requires examination (Odum, 1973; Stockholm Conf. Eco, 1972).

It may be pointed out, quite correctly, that the present situation is developmental, and consequently requires what amounts to a subsidy in fossil-fuel power. When the nuclear-power system is further developed it will contribute an increasing share of electricity. In Great Britain nuclear power now provides 10 percent of the nation's electricity. Nevertheless, nuclear power has been under development in the United States and Britain for nearly 30 years and has been the beneficiary of billions of dollars of government research and development money. No other industry has been so heavily subsidized (Lovins, 1973).

In 1974 in the United States there were 42 nuclear power plants in operation, 56 in various stages of construction, and 101 on order (Lapp, 1974). Most of these were light-water reactors using uranium 235 as fuel. When this undergoes fission it generates enormous amounts of heat. In light-water reactors, water is used to cool the central fuel core. If for any reason water ceased to reach the core, the uranium would heat to 1800° C within a minute. At that temperature the fuel, and the zirconium metal fuel containers would melt. In an hour the whole fuel core would flow to the bottom of the reactor causing steam explosions likely to split the reactor vessel and allow escape of radioactive materials. The core would then continue to burn its way down into the earth, with further escape of radioactivity. To forestall this type of accident, reactors are equipped with an emergency-core-cooling system (ECCS) that floods the reactor if the normal water supply ceased to flow. Unfortunately, this ECCS has not been tested in a real situation, and only now are arrangements being made to perform such tests. Serious questions have been raised about the capability of the system to function under emergency conditions (Lovins, 1973; Nature, 1973).

Light-water reactors produce as end products a variety of wastes including uranium itself, which is not totally consumed, and other elements. Among the latter the most significant is plutonium 239. This is highly poisonous and on burning becomes plutonium oxide, a fine dust that is probably more dangerous to human life than any other substance (McPhee, 1973). Plutonium 239, if controlled, is a fissionable fuel for other types of nuclear plants. All of the radioactive wastes removed from a nuclear plant when the fuel core is recharged, must be disposed of. They are first reprocessed to remove the useful uranium and plutonium, and then the other wastes are stored. Since some of these will remain radioactive for thousands of years, their ultimate disposal presents problems that have not yet been solved to everyone's (or anyone's) satisfaction. The containers in which they are placed must be watched to prevent corrosion and leakage. Ocean dumping brings the risk of radioactive contamination of the marine environment. Land storage, even in caves or mines, is accompanied by the danger that leakage could contaminate ground water supplies. The transportation of these waste products from nuclear-power plant, to reprocessing plant, to storage area is accompanied by risk of accident, sabotage, and other dangers of environmental contamination (Lovins, 1973, Stockholm Conf. Eco, 1972).

During the operation of a light-water reactor, some radioactive materials escape to the atmosphere in flue gases, and some escape to rivers, lakes, or oceans in the heated water that is discharged from the plant. Although the level of radiation released is not considered immediately dangerous, argument continues about the long-term danger of such low-level radioactive wastes (Lewis, 1973; Hedgpeth, 1973).

Another type of nuclear-power plant that is now being brought into use is the high-temperature, gas-cooled reactor. This uses as fuel uranium 235 plus thorium. It is cooled by liquid helium instead of by water and can operate at a higher temperature than water-cooled plants. This provides for greater efficiency in fuel use. The end products contain more fissionable uranium, in the form of uranium 233, than they do plutonium, which leads to less danger in its reprocessing for further use in other plants. This plant is being developed in the United Kingdom and the United States (CEQ, 1973; Patterson, 1972).

Those who favor nuclear-fission power place great hope on the development of liquid-metal, fast-breeder reactors. These can use the common form of uranium (uranium 238) in combination with plutonium as a fuel. They convert uranium 238 into plutonium and thus, theoretically, produce more fuel than they consume—hence the term breeder reactor. They operate at intense heat, and presumably can utilize 60 percent or more of the total energy from uranium, as compared to 2 percent from the light water reactor. The fuel core discharges heat and radioactivity into molten sodium metal, which in turn exchanges heat, but little radioactivity, with another liquid sodium system, which is then used to heat water to generate the steam for the turbines (CEQ, 1973; Nature, 1973).

Early experience with fast breeder reactors has not been encouraging, since both of the pilot models suffered from serious accidents. Although development is planned on a full-scale power plant of this kind, the Atomic Energy Commission has been required by the courts to demonstrate the efficiency and safety of the entire fast-breeder system, rather than considering the impact of a single nuclear plant in isolation. The question of how to safely manage the quantities of plutonium that are produced is not the least difficult of the problems. Even a small amount of this metal, in irresponsible hands, could be a serious menace to humanity. It is, of course, the principal ingredient of the "dirtier" type of atomic bomb.

Many scientists believe that the further development of nuclear-fission power is too fraught with danger to be pursued. The Swedish Nobel-laureate physicist Hannes Alfvén has pointed out that the existing technology leaves no room for either "Acts of God" or normal human frailty, and he states that "we have to conclude that fission energy does not represent an acceptable solution to the energy problem. . . . In general, the breeders are much more dangerous (than present reactors), and current plans to develop breeders should be revised (Stockholm Conf. Eco, 1972)." Nevertheless the Atomic Energy Commission and the nuclear-power industry have an enormous stake in making nuclear-fission energy a success. For them to turn aside and abandon their plans at this point would be to admit that billions of dollars of money and great amounts of scientific and technological expertise have been largely wasted. A determination to push ahead with the development of nuclear-fission power has been demonstrated by governments and private industries, in all countries that have access to the materials and technology. Despite this determination, it is unlikely that nuclear-fission energy is going to provide a quick answer to the world's energy problems. In the words of Amory Lovins (1973): "Nuclear power does not represent a large reservoir of cheap energy capable of being mobilized very simply and quickly; it is on the contrary one of the most complex and unforgiving technologies known to man. Some people still think that nuclear capacity in, say, the USA will increase 250x by (the year) 2000 and that the equivalent of total present US electrical capacity will then be built every 24 months. There is no accounting for what some people think."

Nuclear Fusion. There are many who would prefer to see a large part of the funds now devoted to nuclear-fission technology turned instead to the perfection of the technology for nuclear fusion. Nuclear fusion is regarded by some as the ultimate answer to mankind's energy needs, not just for decades, but forever. The fuel to be used in nuclear fusion is heavy hydrogen, deuterium, which occurs in heavy water, D_2O. This is a normal, but dispersed component of sea water, but is available in virtually unlimited amounts relative to human requirements for fusion fuel. In theory nuclear-fusion reactors cannot get out of control, nor do they create as byproducts or end products materials that can be used to construct atom bombs. The radioactive products produced, such as tritium (3H), would be recycled as fuel. Thus the problem of storing great quantities of dangerously radioactive materials, in theory, does not arise (Lovins, 1973).

Those who favor nuclear fusion as a source of power believe that a practical nuclear-fusion reactor will be built before the end of the century, and thereafter mankind will have unlimited supplies of energy. Others are less optimistic, both about the likelihood of developing a working reactor and also about its contribution to humanity's energy needs. There is no doubt that the technology involved will be far more complicated than fission technology, and hence probably not exportable to countries that lack a well-developed industrial technology. Furthermore, since no working fusion reactor exists it is impossible to fully evaluate safety problems. A fission reactor in theory, can be built that is safe and foolproof, but none are in use because they are not economically practical. The economics of fusion power have been little explored, but one may suspect that economic considerations may result in fusion reactors being built without full regard for safety factors. Furthermore, even assuming that all problems of safety can be overcome and that no dangerous chemical or radioactive pollutants are produced, one by-product of fusion power cannot be removed and will eventually limit the development of all such energy sources—heat. Lovins (1973) has evaluated fusion power in this way: "Some would say that no nuclear source can be clean and safe; and that though nuclear power is admirable when properly sited, the source and user should be rather widely separated—say, about 150 million km." Mankind has one fusion reactor available and in operation that meets Lovins' requirements—the sun.

All sources of power on which industrial civilization relies at the present time, or plans to develop on a large scale in the future, including fossil fuels, fission power, or fusion power contribute heat to the biosphere over and above that normally contributed by the sun. The input of solar energy is over the long run balanced by radiation from the earth's atmosphere with the energy being dispersed through outer space. However, during this process energy is stored in living materials, used to move water into the atmosphere and thus distribute it around the earth, and to maintain atmospheric temperatures at levels generally suitable to living organisms. Since mankind has learned to rely on fossil fuels, and more recently on fission power, additional heat has been added to the biosphere. So far the effects of heat accumulation have been localized. Severe problems of heat pollution develop in water bodies that receive effluent water from fossil-fuel power plants or nuclear plants. So-called heat domes develop over major industrial cities, and these affect local climates. As yet, however, the heat generated by civilization has not been sufficient to cause an overall warming of the earth's atmosphere (SCEP, 1970). If such a warming were to take place, and it were in the order of a few degrees centigrade, climatic changes would occur. These could, for example, result in a melting of the polar ice caps and a flooding of coastal areas throughout the world—the areas where most people live and most cities are located (Lamb, 1974). Such a melting and flooding would no doubt restore the equilibrium. However, if surviving humanity continued to generate fusion power, fission power, or fossil-power at an increasing rate, the earth could be made largely uninhabitable. Thus a heat barrier exists that sets a final limit on energy generation. At what time, or what level of energy use, we would reach that thermal barrier is difficult or impossible to predict. However, to add to the problem, with continued and increasing use of fossil fuels, carbon dioxide is added to the atmosphere. If the CO_2 content of the atmosphere continues to increase, a "greenhouse effect" is likely to occur. The element CO_2, like glass in a greenhouse, will impede the radiation of heat from the earth's surface into space. Combined with increasing generation of heat from fossil fuel and nuclear sources this could lead to a more rapid approach to the thermal barrier than would occur from heat generation alone (SCEP, 1970).

One wonders why we continue to approach this thermal barrier when solar energy and its derivatives—energy from vegetation, from wind, and from moving water—are now little used. Development of these energy sources to meet future needs would add nothing to the heat budget of the earth.

A Compounding of Problems

Thus far, energy needs and availability have been treated only superficially but the complexity of the problem should be obvious. It is difficult to summarize a situation about which so many experts disagree. However, some things are obvious. We have serious energy problems at our present level of population and technology, and these will grow. These problems result not from any overall shortage of energy, but from an unbalanced development of certain types of power (petroleum, nuclear fission), to the neglect of others (solar, wind, geothermal). Furthermore, the energy resources on which civilization has learned to rely, notably petroleum, are distributed around the earth in such a way that political problems of a serious nature tend to arise, and these have, in the past, led to war.

Because of our unbalanced development of energy, we will face within the next few decades a serious energy crisis resulting from the near exhaustion of petroleum and natural gas resources. This can be forestalled by rapid development of alternative power sources, but this process must be started immediately and carried through as rapidly as technology permits. It also can be forestalled, and in a more satisfactory way, by a shift from styles of living that require high energy consumption, and great waste of energy, to life styles less dependent on a high utilization of energy. By either, or preferably both, of these means, petroleum and natural gas reserves can be kept available for those purposes for which they are most essential and for which it is least likely that satisfactory substitutes can be developed.

With the present energy situation, and that which can be immediately foreseen, and with continued population growth, there is no hope that the so-called underdeveloped countries of the world can follow pathways of development leading to a similar pattern of high energy consumption and waste that now characterizes the United States, Europe, and Japan. The pathways for economic development in these countries must be those that make use of other sources of energy and not on a fossil-fuel technology (Spurgeon, 1973).

The present emphasis on rapid development of nuclear fission as an energy source will give rise to an increasing number of problems. Among these are continuing increases in the so-called "low level" pollution of water and atmosphere by radioisotopes released in the effluent of the power plants. Increasing problems will pursue attempts to store and maintain the "high level" radioactive wastes that result from replacement of fuels and their end products. Local problems of thermal pollution will grow more severe and will eventually have more than local effects. It is probable that sooner or later serious accidents will occur in nuclear-fission plants. If these are located near urban areas great loss of human life and other damage will result. Furthermore, in some countries, the distribution of the extremely dangerous plutonium in private hands, and its shipment around the world, will result in its being used in a destructive or threatening way. The danger is not only that it could fall into the hands of criminal or revolutionary groups, but that it is already in the hands of people who are not necessarily reliable. There is no particular reason to believe that private companies, which now possess plutonium, will always remain unwilling to use it for threat or blackmail—particularly if the people choose a government unfriendly to private corporations that threatens their power and profit. A generation that has watched the ramifications of the Watergate scandal in the United States, or has seen the military takeover in Chile in defense of private capital and at the expense of a popularly elected government can hardly rest secure with the accumulation of military power in the hands of private corporations.

To plunge even deeper into the abyss created by our devotion to an energy-wasting way of life and our reliance on fossil fuel and nuclear power, to enable this to continue we need briefly consider once more that our energy use, particularly in the United States, is not static but growing. Furthermore this increased consumption of energy has been considered, by those in the energy business and their government cohorts, as a healthy thing. If energy consumption were to continue to grow at a rate of 5 percent per year, and this has been recommended, then we would reach the final dilemma. Lovins (1973) has pointed out that if we could manage the impossible and *build one massive nuclear power plant every day* for the rest of this century, we would still be dependent in the year 2000 on fossil fuels to provide more than half of our primary industrial energy demand. Obviously, this is not the way to go.

Alternative Energy Resources

For the long term the greatest hope lies in adopting an energy-conserving way of life combined with the development of renewable, nonfissionable, energy resources. Such a development and way of life could permit a reasonably high material standard of living for a human population willing to limit its numbers and its consumption of material resources to some level that the earth can continue to support.

Let us consider briefly a few of these renewable or inexhaustible sources of energy.

Geothermal Energy.   Development of this source has been limited to volcanically active regions. Thus Iceland heats approximately half of its homes geothermally, New Zealand's North Island derives one fifth of its electricity from geothermal sources, and one geothermal plant in North Italy generates half the power needed to run the country's railroad system. Spurgeon (1973) has estimated that 20 percent of the electrical needs of the United States in 1985 could be derived from geothermal sources. Abrahamson (1973) however, points out that much research and development must go into this area, since at present geothermal power is derived from dry steam or hot water. To make this a major energy source we must learn to tap the energy from hot, dry rocks that are more widely distributed in the earth's crust. He nevertheless believes it possible that 100,000 megawatts of geothermal electrical generating capacity could be deployed in the United States by the end of the century. This is equivalent to the potential of 100 large (1000 million watt) nuclear power plants.

Wind Power.   Abrahamson has pointed out that the WMO reports that there are 20 million megawatts of wind power available to wind generators, assuming a conservative degree of placement of these generators. He further notes that in the Great Plains alone, assuming a reasonable spacing of wind generators, there could be an electrical generating capacity of 200,000 megawatts (equal to 200 large nuclear power plants). Wind power, however, appears to make most sense when it is used locally. One small wind generator, of the type developed in Australia, has been noted as supplying all of the power needs of a 50-acre farm, without interruption (see *Mother Earth News Almanac,* 1973). Wind power, also, can be used to do work, directly, in pumping water, turning mill wheels, and the like, without the power waste involved in electricity generation (McCaull, 1973).

Solar Power. Considering that a terawatt equals one trillion or 10^{12} watts, we may note that 350,000 terawatt-hours of solar power reach the earth in each year. This is too large a figure to comprehend. Hall (1974) has pointed out that if the solar radiation impinging on the United States could be converted to electricity at an efficiency rate of 10 percent, then 1.5 percent of the land surface could supply all of the energy needs of the country at the present time. Photochemical conversion to produce electricity has achieved at least 14 percent efficiency, but is still an expensive and relatively little developed process. Odum (1973) is of the opinion that the energy waste in generating electricity from such a diffuse energy source as sunlight would be too great to make the process profitable. However, solar roofs, and other forms of solar collectors, which do not necessarily produce electricity, can be used and are being used effectively (Fig. 8). If these were widely employed they would virtually eliminate the need for any other source of power for space heating of homes or other buildings. This alone would remove a major drain on other energy resources. Furthermore, as Spurgeon (1973) has pointed out, solar power can be used directly in processing municipal or agricultural waste into methane gas that can then be used to fuel vehicles or to supply gas burners for cooking and heating. The potentials for the use of solar power have been widely neglected, but it is safe to say that either directly or indirectly solar radiation is the sanest and most reliable source of energy for mankind's future. Further consideration to this and other promising energy sources will be given in the chapters that follow.

Metals and Minerals

To shift from a consideration of energy resources to that of other material resources is to encounter the same areas of confusion. Technological civilization, more than any that preceded it, has become a consumer of ever-growing numbers of *things*. These things must be supplied if technological civilization is to continue along the lines that it has been going. However, it is impossible to supply them in the quantities that will be required if growth continues and technological civilization is to spread its "benefits" evenly around the world. In other words, if we try to supply all of humanity in the way that the people of the technologically advanced countries are now supplied we will fail in this effort. There are not enough things to go around. Human requirements, however, are not the same as the requirements for people living in technological

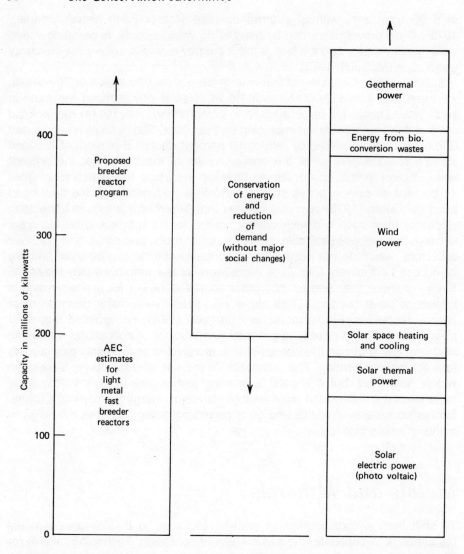

figure 8

Alternative ways for reaching the same energy goal, based on energy "requirements" for the United States in 2000 A.D. Notice that a reasonable development of nonconventional energy resources can produce more power than the proposed breeder reactor program. A reasonable conservation of energy can greatly reduce the demand for this additional power. Data from Scientists Institute for Public Information (Gillette, R., 1974, *Science, 184*:650–651).

civilization. Living at a more simple cultural level, humanity could get along reasonably well without a high consumption of material resources. Since most of the material resources required by technological civilization are nonrenewable we must find ways to make their supply last longer. These ways will include substitution of relatively abundant, or renewable resources, for scarce nonrenewable resources, and reuse or recycling of those minerals that are already available and in circulation.

If we examine the existing levels of use, projected future levels of use, and available supplies of minerals we once again encounter problems in terminology. Most minerals occur in the earth in the form of *ores* in which the mineral under consideration will usually exist in various chemical combinations and mixtures with other minerals. A mineral deposit is known as an ore only if the mineral exists in such concentration and quantity that it can be extracted profitably under the technological and economic conditions that exist, or can be foreseen for the short-term future. Thus an increase in the price of a metal will cause an increase in the available ores. *Reserves* of minerals are the sum of those ores known to exist, or that can be reasonably inferred to exist (because of known geological conditions). *Potential ores* and reserves are those that would become available if prices and technology change in favorable directions (Landsberg, 1964).

It is instructive to once again consider the figures provided by Meadows et al. in *The Limits to Growth*. In the table that follows various forecasts are shown: the lifetime of existing reserves at present rates of consumption; the lifetime of these reserves, assuming that past growth in the rate of consumption continues into the future; the lifetime, also assuming a continuing growth in rate of consumption, if existing reserves are 5 times greater than expected; and the percentage of total world consumption represented by United States consumption of that mineral. Minerals are listed in order of their probable time of depletion.

These statistics are depressing for one who is concerned with the future of technological civilization. Before discussing them it is worthwhile to compare them with the estimates of other authorities. Preston Cloud (1969) sees shortages developing within 20 years for gold, silver, tin, zinc, lead, platinum, and uranium 235 and finds that by the year 2042 we would only be able to count on continuing supplies of iron, manganese, chromium, nickel, molybdenum, cobalt, and aluminum, plus those materials that can be derived from sea water. Even these relatively abundant metals would not meet world demands if rates of consumption increase throughout the world to high levels. Milner Schaefer (1970) calls attention to the relative abundance of manganese, cobalt, nickel, copper, zinc, and phosphates in deposits on the ocean floor, but cautions that the technology may not become available to make them contribute in a major way to the world's needs. J. H. Westbrook (1970), however, looking at the situation from a metallurgist's viewpoint is optimistic and bases this on

Mineral	Number of Years Supply Under Existing Rate of Use (1970)	Number of Years Supply Assuming Continued Growth in Rate of Use	Assuming Reserves Are 5 Times Those Now Known	U.S. Percent of Total World Consumption
Gold	11	9	29	26
Mercury	13	13	41	24
Silver	16	13	42	24
Tin	17	15	61	22
Zinc	23	18	50	26
Copper	36	21	48	33
Lead	26	21	64	25
Tungsten	40	28	72	22
Aluminum	100	31	55	42
Molybdenum	79	34	65	40
Manganese	97	46	94	14
Platinum	130	47	85	31
Nickel	150	53	96	38
Cobalt	110	60	148	32
Chromium	420	95	154	19
Iron	240	93	173	28

"intensified exploration, improved prospecting techniques, more efficient means of production, and intersubstitution of materials."

The Ecologist, using an approach similar to that of Meadows and associates, has calculated the length of time before present reserves of minerals are exhausted, assuming both current (1970) rates of use, and exponential growth in the rate of use equivalent to that between 1960 and 1968. Under these conditions it is found that the reserves of silver, gold, copper, mercury, molybdenum, lead, nickel, platinum, tin, and zinc will be largely exhausted before 2000 AD. Reserves of aluminum, cobalt, manganese, and tungsten will be used by 2020 AD. Only iron and chromium, among the metals that are considered, will last beyond 2040 AD. (*The Ecologist,* 1972).

Westbrook has noted that the number of metals consumed on a major scale in the United States in 1970 was 11 and would probably grow to 17 by the year 2000. Of these, 7 are considered by Cloud and Meadows, et al. as likely to be largely exhausted by the year 2000.

In examining the table in *The Limits to Growth* it is worth noting that the lion's share of most minerals is consumed by the United States. If the United States were to be accepted as the manufacturing center for the world, these figures would not be particularly disturbing. However, importation of minerals, paying very little to the producing country, followed by export at high cost of manufactured materials, allows the people of the United States to live at an extremely high material standard compared to that of the major mineral-producing countries. Following the examples set by the oil-producing nations, the mineral producing nations may be expected to raise prices in order to obtain a greater share of the world's wealth, now, and to maintain levels of production based, not on the demands of the consumer nations, but on provision for their own long-term well-being. The days of cheap, raw materials, whether fuels or other minerals, are virtually over. The world will have to readjust its economy to account for this change.

Principal Producing Country	Metals Produced with Percentage of Total World Production	
U.S.S.R.	Chromium	30
	Copper	15
	Iron	25
	Lead	13
	Manganese	34
	Mercury	18
	Nickel	16
	Platinum	59
	Tungsten	19
	Zinc	11
United States	Copper	20
	Iron	14
	Molybdenum	64
	Tungsten	14
	Zinc	8
South Africa	Gold	77
	Manganese	13
Canada	Gold	6
	Lead	11
	Molybdenum	14
	Nickel	42
	Silver	20
	Zinc	23

The source of most of the world's mineral wealth is worth examining, and is based also on the data from Meadows et al.

In addition to these four major producers of two or more metals the following countries reach distinction from their production of particular metals: Jamaica 19 percent of world's aluminum; Zaire, 51 percent of cobalt; Spain, 22 percent of mercury; New Caledonia, 28 percent of nickel; Malaysia, 41 percent of tin; and China 25 percent of tungsten. The supply of chromium in Rhodesia has created political problems since countries that have little chromium, such as the United States, have been willing to disregard the United Nations' sanctions against this country in order to obtain chromium. By contrast, the U.S.S.R., rich in chromium, has been able to take a righteous attitude toward this behavior. Zaire, Zambia, Brazil, Jamaica, Mexico, Peru, Malaysia, Bolivia, Thailand, Chile, and Guinea may all be expected in the future to take advantage of their favorable position as metal producers to demand a larger share of the world's wealth. The countries that will suffer most from this squeeze are those that have neither economic wealth nor mineral resources.

Each new increase in price will bring into production new mineral ores that were previously considered economically unprofitable. However, such low-grade ores require far more energy expenditure in their mining and processing than the ores previously used. It has been pointed out by some experts that all of the world's mineral needs could be supplied, potentially, from the mining of common rock, and the distillation of sea water. This would be true under two conditions, that virtually unlimited cheap energy was available, and that some means could be found for disposing of the enormous quantities of waste products that would be the result of such processing. Presumably, if energy were cheap and abundant enough, the latter problem could be solved since we could build new mountain ranges or make new islands in the sea. However, since unlimited, cheap energy is not going to be available within the next 30 years and probably will never be available, it is pointless to discuss this possibility. Even now, our need to process the ores being mined today places a great drain on energy resources.

For the next few decades we must face the fact that we will run very low on some elements that have been essential to urban-industrial civilization. To compensate we are going to have to reduce consumption of these materials, we are going to have to reuse, or recycle scrap and used metals, and we are going to have to find substitutes. Fortunately recycling of metals need not be energy intensive, and in comparison with mining and concentrating ever leaner ores, can be energy saving (Lovins, 1973).

If the human race is going to have a future extending much beyond the next 100 years, it is going to have to forsake "civilization as we have known it," and find some less wasteful means of living within the limited resources of the biosphere.

For those nations that had hoped to develop levels of material and energy consumption equivalent to those that have recently prevailed in the United States the message is that there is *no way* for this to happen. In the words of Preston Cloud:

"It can be calculated that this would require keeping in circulation more than 60 billion tons of iron, about a billion tons of lead (not allowing for battery operated automobiles), around 700 million tons of zinc, and more than 50 million tons of tin—or between 200 and 400 times present world annual production of these commodities. . . . As it is not possible to increase metal production by anywhere near the suggested amounts by the end of the century, if ever, rising expectations among the deprived peoples of the earth that they too may share the affluent life are doomed to bitter disappointment without population control and eventual reduction in population to its present or lower level."

Food

During the years following World War II sweeping changes in agricultural practices took place in the United States and through much of the industrialized world. Farm labor and farm livestock were replaced by machinery, heavy applications of chemical fertilizer were employed, the use of herbicides to control weeds, and pesticides to control insects and other agricultural pests was to become a normal part of agricultural practice. New hybrid plants especially bred to take advantage of the new farm conditions took the place of earlier breeds. Irrigation became much more widespread, even on farms in humid regions, to prevent any danger that water shortage would temporarily restrict growth. The result of all of these practices was a phenomenal increase in agricultural yields. The United States became an important food supplier to the world, and for a time stockpiles of grain and other foodstuffs grew to such a level that they were a national source of embarrassment in a hungry world. Acres devoted to farm production declined, and more land became available for forestry, wildlife, recreation or urban purposes. Farm laborers decreased from 32 million in 1935 to 9 million in 1970 during a period when the total United States population was increasing by 50 percent. Working livestock on farms declined even more sharply.

The new agricultural technology was soon to be spread to developing countries. In Mexico the Rockefeller Foundation sponsored an agricultural improvement program that made use of the new techniques along with improved varieties of corn and wheat. The results were spectacular. In 1941 Mexico had produced only 50 percent of the wheat that its people consumed. By 1960, despite a marked increase in population, Mexico was self-sufficient in wheat. Equally spectacular gains were made in corn production.

In the late 1960s and the 1970s, the Food and Agricultural Organization of the United Nations along with other development agencies launched the

Green Revolution. Taking advantage of the Mexican hybrid grains, and other high-yield wheats, along with a new high-yield rice developed by the International Rice Research Institute in the Philippines, and making use of modern technology, grain outputs were tripled in some areas, and great increases in yield were reported from Kenya, Pakistan, India, the Philippines, and elsewhere. For a time, some agricultural experts believed that the world food problem was within reach of a "final" solution and that it would be possible to boost food yields faster than population growth for some years to come (Dasmann, 1972).

New problems, however, were to develop. New breeds of grain grown in extensive monocultures provided a happy hunting ground for new crop diseases and insect pests. In 1970, for example, a new variety of the southern corn leaf blight wiped out 10 percent of the field-corn crop in the Middle Western United States. Plant breeders were hard pressed to develop new resistant varieties. Plant pests showed their expected ability to adjust to pesticides by the development of pesticide-resistant populations. In 1972 and 1973, the effects of dry years were felt both in the failure of needed rainfall and the lowered availability of water for irrigation. Talk of famine was again heard, and Norman Borlaug, "father of the Green Revolution" and Nobel Prize winner for his efforts, warned that 20 million people might die because of crop shortages during 1974-1975.

The principal reason for the slowdown in the agricultural revolution, however, is revealed in studies such as those carried out by David Pimentel and his associates (1973). In these studies he measured the energy inputs required to produce an acre of corn, using the modern agricultural techniques of the United States. The results are as shown at top of page 65.

It will be noted that labor is the smallest single calorie input, whereas fertilizers, gasoline, machinery, electricity, and the cost of drying and transportation dominate the energy input. Pimentel, et al., compare the situation between 1945, when labor inputs were much higher, and 1970, and find a marked decrease in energy yield in relation to energy input, from 3.70 to 1 in 1945 down to 2.82 in 1970. It would be far more instructive to examine the ratio at the time the plow first "broke the plains," when there was no input of fertilizer except for animal manure, no gasoline, little machinery, no electricity, no insecticides or herbicides, but instead a high input of human and animal labor.

The energy budget of Pimentel and associates is based on corn, which is not one of the more energy-demanding crops, even though its production is fully mechanized. Furthermore, the budget does not take into account all of the other energy costs involved in processing corn, transporting it, packaging it, and finally getting it to the consumer. Since the consumer is often a steer or a hog, a further energy loss comes in the conversion of corn to beef or pork. A more detailed analysis of this process was carried out by Eric Hirst (1973) who estimated that in 1970, two quadrillion kilocalories or 12 percent

Energy Inputs Per Acre of Corn Produced, United States, 1970.

Input	Kilocalories of Energy
Fertilizer (Nitrogen)	940,800
Gasoline	797,000
Machinery	420,000
Electricity	310,000
Drying	120,000
Transportation	70,000
Fertilizer (Potassium)	68,000
Seeds planted	63,000
Fertilizer (Phosphorus)	47,100
Irrigation	34,000
Insecticides	11,000
Herbicides	11,000
Labor (21,770 cal/man week of 40 hr)	4900
Total input:	2,896,800
Total output, corn yield	8,164,800
Ratio kilocalorie return/input kcal	2.82

of the total energy used in the United States, were used in providing and preparing food. His energy budget is as follows.

	Per Person, United States, 1970 Millions of Kilocalories
Direct farm use in food production	1.5
Food processing	2.7
Transportation	0.2
Wholesale-retail trade	1.3
Home processing and cooking	2.5
Total energy input	8.2
Energy provided by food consumed	1.1

Obviously the ratio of calorie input to calorie output is more than 7 to 1, hardly a profitable endeavor in energy terms.

Borgstrom (1973) examined this problem and concluded that many western farmers employ, directly on the farm, far more energy than their crops collect—thus for Iowa soy beans the ratio was from 2.35 to 3.5 to 1. Perelman (1972) has evaluated all United States food production and concluded that the energy input, on the farms, was five times the output, whereas by contrast in China, in wet-rice farming, 50 calories are gained in food for every one calorie employed in producing it.

These energy facts, applied to the poor countries of the world and combined with the energy crisis, have caused a retreat from the Green Revolution. The would-be developing countries of the world, for the most part, cannot afford the new high-priced petroleum used to fuel the Green Revolution and produce its fertilizers, insecticides, and herbicides.

There are, however, further consequences of the agricultural revolution which need consideration. Not only is agricultural labor driven off the farms, to seek work in the cities, but the small farmer is driven out of business, at least in those enterprises that require massive use of farm machinery and other expensive inputs. New "agrobusinesses" tend to dominate the agricultural landscape, often owned by corporations with many interests other than farming. This creates problems in the wealthy industrialized countries, but can create tragedies in the poor countries where there is no work and no place to live in the cities, and where the best, and irrigable land is quickly acquired by the large, wealthy agriculturalists, leaving the poor farmer, once again, to scratch a subsistence living from marginal land, unable even to afford the high-priced outputs of the Green Revolution.

Pimentel (1973) further points out that it took 3.3 billion gallons of gasoline to produce the United States corn crop in 1940, and 7.6 billion gallons in 1969. One needs question very seriously if this is really the way to provide for the world food needs. Instead one need examine the practicability of a solar-powered, wind-powered, labor-intensive, livestock-fertilized, and live-horse powered farm as representing a more viable model for the future.

The world, in theory, has devoted a major effort since World War II to boost food supplies at a faster rate than the growth of population. There have been successes, and periods when good cheer prevailed, but the overall record in the developing world is not one of success. In 1972-1973 the surpluses of grain in the United States were used to rescue those countries in which crop failure was pronounced. Now there is no surplus to speak of, and in 1974 the United States will import great quantities of Canadian wheat. Who is going to export food in the future?

The year 1973 was a particularly depressing one for the technological optimists everywhere. Not only was there an energy crisis and widespread crop failures, but the failure of the world's most important ocean fishery also became apparent. For almost 20 years, since the first anchovy fishery was developed off the coast of Peru, world fisheries yields have shown a steady increase, up to a total of around 70 million tons in 1970. This increase was widely heralded as evidence of the ability of ocean fisheries to provide a growing share of world protein needs, and future yields of 100 million or more tons were predicted. It was not generally noticed, however, that the increase in world ocean fishery yields was largely attributable to the growing catch of Peruvian anchovies. By 1968 the Peruvian yield had reached 12 million metric tons, and if this amount were subtracted from the world fishery statistics it would be found that there had actually been a decrease in yield, everywhere else, between 1958 and 1968. In 1972 the anchovy fishery failed. The world was forced to face up to a decline in fishery production. It had been known, but was usually not discussed, that the northeast Atlantic fishery, of major importance to Europe, had declined by one half between 1958 and 1968 (Dasmann, 1972; Loftas, 1972).

The failure of the Peruvian fishery was predictable, since periodically there is a change in oceanographic conditions off the South American coast. Normally prevailing offshore winds, from the deserts, push surface water back from the coast, allowing an upwelling of deep waters, cold and rich in nutrients. These support the plankton that support the fish. Anchovies normally live in cold, upwelling water. However, every now and then, at unpredictable intervals, the cold upwelling fails and the warm water of the Ecuador Current moves down off the shore. This condition, known as *El Niño*, has disastrous effects on all forms of life that depend on the cold upwelling current. However, in 1972 the effects of *El Niño* added to the effects of nearly twenty years of increasingly heavy fishing. It was not known whether the anchovy fishery would recover or follow the path of the once productive California sardine fishery. The latter also had once been one of the great contributors to the fish supplies of the world, but a combination of heavy fishing and changes in oceanographic conditions brought about its failure, and in twenty years it has not recovered (Loftas, 1972).

One could go further to discuss failure in world fishery management and mention the fate of the Atlantic salmon, or of the right whales, blue whales, humpback whales, and fin whales. This would only be depressing. There is little in the way of oceanic fishery management. Instead there is world fishery exploitation, under very little control, because the oceans remain "no man's waters," and all nations have their hallowed sovereign rights to do what they please (Fig. 9).

The fate of other renewable resources, forest resources, forage resources for livestock production, and wildlife resources will be discussed in other chapters. Suffice to say, at this point, that no cheer will be derived from this discussion. Still less would be derived from a consideration of the management of fresh-water resources. The human race has the ecological knowledge to allow for a satisfactory job of managing most renewable resources. For political, economic, and social reasons—or more correctly, excuses—it is failing to do so.

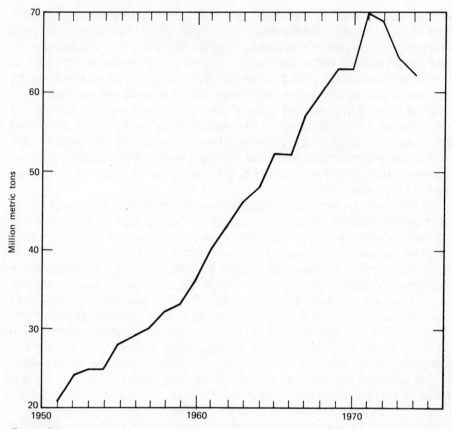

figure 9
World fisheries catch, 1950 to 1973. Much of the decline after 1970 is attributable to
the failure of the Peruvian anchovy fishery. Data from Brown, 1974, p. 46.

Population

According to figures provided by the Population Reference Bureau, Washington, D.C., in the middle of 1973 the population of the world was estimated
at 3,860,000,000 people. Such a figure, taken in isolation, is meaningful only
to population watchers. We also are told that this population, worldwide, was
increasing at a rate of 2 percent per annum, and could be expected to double,
therefore, in 35 years. In other words, by 2008 AD the world population might
reach a level of 7,720,000,000 people. Planners and futurologists who are
considering problems of how to meet the needs of humanity for food, minerals,

energy, and so forth, are at present planning for a population of 7 billion people to be reached during or near the year 2000. And so it would, if present trends continue (Fig. 10).

World populations increase when birth rates exceed death rates (Fig. 10). Birth rates (live births per 1000 people) were 33 in 1973, death rates only 13, leaving an average gain of 20 people per thousand, or 2 percent. Death rates have been lowered drastically in most parts of the world, particularly during the past 3 decades when the control of disease and improvements of sanitation became a major concern of civilization. Death control has been a feature of technological civilization and economic development. However, in earlier years, before the nineteenth century, birth rates and death rates were in rough balance in most parts of the world, excepting the then industrialized countries, and probably fluctuated between 45 and 52 per thousand. The effects of medical technology, improved food, and sanitation has been to reduce the death rate, but not the birth rate. In Africa, with some exceptions, birth rates still range between 45 and 52 and average at 46 per thousand. Death rates, however, have been reduced and even in the most backward countries (Portugal's African colonies) do not exceed 30 per thousand. In Middle America and Tropical South America, and in southern Asia approximately the same situation prevails, however, death rates have been reduced to a lower level than in tropical Africa.

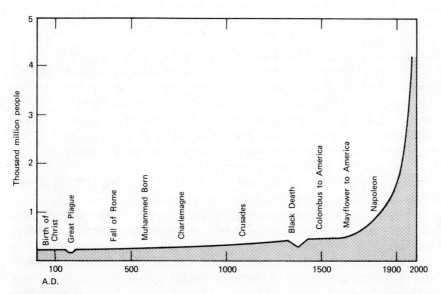

figure 10
World population growth. Based on United Nations estimates and other sources.

The greater part of the world's population growth is taking place in the areas where reduction of death rate has not yet been matched by a reduction in birth rate. The 17 countries with the highest rate of population growth are as follows (Population Reference Bureau).

	Birth Rate	Death Rate	Growth Rate
Kuwait	43	7	9.8
Bahamas	28	6	4.6
Morocco	50	16	3.4
Rhodesia	48	14	3.4
Iraq	49	15	3.4
Dominican Republic	49	15	3.4
Colombia	45	11	3.4
Ecuador	45	11	3.4
Venezuela	41	8	3.4
Paraguay	45	11	3.4
Algeria	50	17	3.3
Jordan	48	15	3.3
Syria	48	15	3.3
Pakistan	51	18	3.3
Phillipines	45	12	3.3
Thailand	43	10	3.3
Honduras	49	17	3.3

With the exception of Kuwait and Bahamas, in which the growth rate is determined by immigration rather than entirely by the difference between births and deaths, all of these countries retain a "primitive" high birth rate accompanied by a much more modern death rate. Most of the developing countries of Africa, Asia, and Latin America do not join this upper group because death rates are still relatively high. Should these be reduced to correspond to the countries listed here, then the population growth worldwide would jump to a much higher rate than the present 2 percent.

For comparison it is worth examining the statistics from the 10 most slowly growing national populations (Population Reference Bureau).

All of these countries have essentially dropped out of the world population race and have achieved near stable populations (Malta, the exception, qualifies only because of its high emigration rate). Indeed, this condition generally applies throughout Western and Northern Europe where growth rates average 0.4, and is being approached in Eastern Europe (growth rate 0.7) and the United States (0.8). No Asian, African, or Latin American nation approaches this level of near stability, except unfortunate Gabon where high death rates and temporarily low birth rates also give it a growth of only 0.8.

	Birth Rate	Death Rate	Growth Rate
Germany (East)	11.7	13.7	−0.2
Malta	16.8	9.1	−0.1
Luxembourg	11.8	11.9	0.0
Germany (West)	11.5	11.7	0.0
Austria	13.8	12.6	0.1
Belgium	13.8	12.0	0.2
Finland	12.7	9.6	0.3
Sweden	13.8	10.4	0.3
United Kingdom	14.9	11.9	0.3
Hungary	14.7	11.4	0.3

Death rates as low as 5 to 7 per thousand characterize countries with young populations, good nutrition, and high levels of medical care and sanitation. Levels of 9 to 11 per thousand characterize most European and North American countries with older populations but similar high levels of nutrition, medical care, and sanitation.

One final statistic before the significance of all of these statistics is discussed: the countries with the highest rates of population growth are those with the lowest per capita incomes (often the gross national product is as low as 60 to 90 dollars per person per year). The reverse is true of the countries with the lowest population growth rate (e.g. 4,760 dollars per person per year in the United States). The exceptions to this rule are the oil-rich Arab states where the high per capita income has not filtered down to the general public in the form of increased public education or direct economic benefits that might lead to the reduction in family size.

It took nearly 200 years, from 1650 to 1850 for the world population to double and reach a level of slightly over one billion. It took 100 years, roughly from 1850 to 1950, for it to double again. It now takes 35 years, and this time could decrease if death control in Asia, Africa, and Latin America becomes more effective. This is the familiar pattern of exponential growth. It is a pattern that cannot be continued for very long, in nature, nor is there any human way in which such growth can be prolonged. Populations will level off, either because people decide, as they seem to have in Europe and the United States that the production of large families brings a decrease in their own and everyone else's well being, or because the means for keeping people alive becomes less available. When the latter happens death rates once again soar to high levels. The human race can decide to slow down its growth rate as a deliberate means of enhancing the well being of everyone, or it can continue to grow, for a while longer. If it continues to grow then one of the following will happen, or some combination of the three: (1) there will be increased mortality resulting from malnutrition and starvation, with some resulting decrease in natality; (2)

there will be increased mortality from disease (operating directly from the effects of malnutrition, or as a consequence of overcrowding, breakdown of sanitation, and lack of medical care;) or (3) there will be increased mortality resulting from crime and warfare. There are no other alternatives.

It has already been noted that an increasing scarcity of energy resources, accompanied by higher prices, is not likely to be relieved (if ever) much before the year 2000. This will have particularly severe effects on the poorer countries with the higher population growth rates. It has been noted that the world is running out of essential mineral resources, and that the prospects for the poorer countries to achieve levels of material consumption equivalent to those of the rich countries, are slim indeed. It further has been noted that the prospects for increasing world food supplies faster than present rates of population growth are less than bright, and with increasing scarcity of mineral and energy resources are becoming dim. This means that instead of an improving diet, more people will try to get along with less. Already there have been significant starvation losses, accompanied by threats of even more severe losses of people in the near future. Good growth years and bountiful crops could provide some temporary alleviation, but only temporary if human population growth rates continue along present levels.

Perhaps the most dismal news in the world population area is the general failure of voluntary birth control programs to become effective, except in the wealthy countries where levels of public education and economic well being are high (Table 2). In the developing world it is not only difficult to reach people with the information and means that would encourage birth control, but far too many national governments have developed a semiparanoic attitude toward the subject, viewing any attempt at population limitation as some sort of neocolonialist plot. For voluntary birth control programs to become effective it is not only necessary to convince individuals of the need for birth control, and the personal benefits they will derive from smaller families, it is also necessary to see to it that such personal benefits do result, and to have a deliberate national policy that favors maintaining low levels of population growth. For most of the countries of the developing world this seems out of reach for some time to come. [For a fuller elaboration of this problem see Hardin (1972).]

It is not that governments have failed to solve the problem of achieving a better balance between populations and resources. Unfortunately, with few exceptions, they have not even addressed this problem. Instead there is a blind faith in science and technology, combined with a determination to avoid facing unpleasant facts. There is a willingness to pay lip service to the idea of aid for developing countries, combined with some token provision of real assistance. However the amount spent on international aid by the rich countries has never been sufficient to accomplish the stated objectives, and is completely trivial in comparison to military budgets. Furthermore, since most international aid is motivated by the same blind belief in the value of continued economic

table 2
Population policy positions directly influencing fertility

PRONATALIST Use of contraceptives prohibited	Examples of Practicing Nations None
Contraceptive sales illegal	Ireland, Spain
Contraceptive sales allowed, advertising illegal	Argentina, Malta
Pronatalist incentives offered: income tax deductions for children; maternity benefits, child allowances, public housing preference, scholarships	France, Romania, Bulgaria, Czechoslovakia, Hungary
LAISSEZ FAIRE Pronatalist	Israel, U.S.S.R., Brazil
Neutral	Switzerland, Italy, Chad, Burma, Saudi Arabia
Antinatalist	Liberia, Iraq
ANTINATALIST Government support of private family planning	Australia, Belgium, Canada, German Federal Republic
Official government family planning	Denmark, Norway, Sweden, Japan, United Kingdom. United States
Official family programme plus motivation campaign, advertising, education, etc.	Egypt, Kenya, Colombia, Bangladesh, Indonesia, Iran
Official family planning plus stronger measures: e.g., economic incentives, curtailment of privileges, restraints on marriage, restrictions on number of children	China, India, Singapore
POLICIES TOWARD INDUCED ABORTIONS Prohibited without exception	Ireland, Belgium, Portugal, Bolivia, Panama, Indonesia
Permitted for medical reasons only	France, Italy, Switzerland, Algeria, Kenya, Peru
Permitted for social reasons only	Jordan
Permitted for medical or social reasons	Sweden, United Kingdom, Japan, Australia, Cuba, India
Elective (without legal restriction by Government)	U.S.S.R., Austria, Denmark, United States, China, Tunisia

Source. World Bank Staff Report, 1974. Population policies and economic development. Johns Hopkins University Press, Baltimore, 214 pp.

and population growth its total effect has probably been more harmful than good.

The belief in continuing growth is like a near-fatal disease that has spread from technological civilization to infect all parts of the world it has touched. One cannot hope for an immediate cure, but one can hope that its progress can be arrested until a cure can be found.

The World's Largest Countries 1973 (Population Reference Bureau)

	Population	Growth Rate (per 1000)	Per Capita GNP (dollars)
China	799,300,000	17	160
India	600,400,000	25	110
U.S.S.R.	250,000,000	10	1790
United States	210,300,000	8	4760
Indonesia	132,500,000	29	80
Japan	107,300,000	12	1920
Brazil	101,300,000	28	420
Pakistan	68,300,000	33	100
Nigeria	59,600,000	26	120
West Germany	59,400,000	00	2930

References

Abrahamson, Dean, 1973. Energy technology: status and needs. *Ambio*, 2:186–195.

Borgstrom, Georg, 1973. Food, feed and energy. *Ambio*, 2:214–219.

Brown, Lester R., 1973. Grubbing for earth's crust. *The Guardian*, London, Dec. 5, p. 16.

Cloud, Preston, 1969. *Resources, population and quality of life.* University of California, Santa Barbara, Mimeo.

Council on Environmental Quality (CEQ), 1973. *Energy and the environment. Electric power.* U. S. Government, Washington, D.C.

———, 1973. *Environmental quality.* U. S. Government, Washington, D.C.

Dahlberg, Kenneth A., 1973. Towards a policy of zero energy growth. *Ecologist*, 3:338–341.

Dasmann, R. F., 1972. *Environmental conservation*, 3rd ed., John Wiley, New York.

Ecologist, 1972. Blueprint for survival. *Ecologist*, 2:1–43.

Forbes, Ian; D.F. Ford; H.W. Kendall, and J.J. Mackenzie, 1972. Cooling water. *Environment*, 14: 40–47.

Gillette, Robert, 1973. Nuclear safeguards: holes in the fence. *Science, 182*:1112–1114.

———, 1973. Western coal: does the debate follow irreversible commitment? *Science, 182*: 456–458.

Hall, John, 1974. Bright ideas. *Nature, 247*:331.

Hardin, Garret, 1972. *Exploring new ethics for survival. The voyage of the space ship Beagle*. Viking, New York.

Hedgpeth, Joel, 1973. Environment, power and pollution. *Quarterly Review of Biology, 48*:19–21.

Hirst, Eric, 1973. Living off the fuels of the land. *Natural History, 82*:20–22.

Lamb, Hubert H., 1974. Is the earth's climate changing? *Ecologist, 4*:10–15.

Landsberg, H. H., 1964. *Natural resources for U.S. growth*. Johns Hopkins, Baltimore.

Lapp, Ralph E., 1974. Nuclear safety—the public debate. *New Scientist, 61*:394–396.

Leach, Gerald, 1973. Transport moves off oil. *New Scientist, 60*:396–400.

Lewis, Richard, 1973. Shippingport—the killer reactor? *New Scientist, 59*:552–553.

Loftas, Tony, 1972. Where have all the anchoveta gone? *New Scientist, 58*:583–586.

Lovins, Amory B., 1973. *World energy strategies: facts, issues, and options*.

MacKillop, Andrew, 1973. Living off the sun. *Ecologist, 3*:260–265.

McCaull, Julian, 1973. Windmills. *Environment, 15*:6–17.

McPhee, John, 1973. The curve of binding energy. *New Yorker*, Dec. 3:54–145; Dec. 10: 50–108; Dec. 17: 60–97.

Meadows, D. H., et al., 1972. *The limits to growth*. Signet, New American Library, New York.

Mende, Tiber, 1973. *From aid to recolonization. Lessons of a failure*. Harrap, London.

Mother Earth News Almanac, 1973. Bantam Books, New York.

Nature, 1973. Britain to buy LW reactors from U. S. *Nature, 246*:181–182.

———, 1973. Oil from shale: answer to the energy crisis. *Nature, 246*:323–324.

Norman, Colin, 1974. Geothermal energy in California. *Nature, 247*:81.

Novick, Sheldon, 1973. Toward a nuclear power precipice. *Environment, 15*:32–40.

Oakley, Donald T., 1972. *Natural radiation exposure in the United States*. Environmental Protection Agency, Washington.

Patterson, Walter, 1972. U. S. ponders possible runaway reactors. *New Scientist, 55*:476–478.

Perelman, M. J., 1972. Farming with petroleum. *Environment, 14*:8–11.

Pimentel, David, et al., 1973. Food production and the energy crisis. *Science, 182*:443–449.

Schaefer, Milner, 1970. *The resources base and prospective rates of development in relation to planning requirements*. Mimeo. Center for Study of Democratic Institutions, Santa Barbara, Calif.

Odum, Howard T., 1973. Energy, ecology, and economics. *Ambio, 2*:220–227.

Study of Critical Environmental Problems (SCEP), 1970. *Man's impact on the global environment*. Massachusetts Institute of Technology, Cambridge.

Spurgeon, David, 1973. Natural power for the Third World. *New Scientist, 60*:694–697.

Sterba, James P., 1974. U. S. stimulates development of rich oil deposit in west. *International Herald Tribune*, Jan. 7.

Stockholm Conference Eco, 1972. Atomic reactor safety hearings. *Stockholm Conference Eco*, Washington, Aug. 11–Sept. 8.

Tamplin, Arthur R., 1973. Solar energy. *Environment, 15*:16–20, 32–34.

Westbrook, J. H., 1970. Materials for tomorrow. *Science and technology in the world of the future*. Wiley-Interscience, New York.

Whittemore, F. Case, 1973. How much in reserve? *Environment, 15*:16–20, 31–35.

Wilkes, H. Garrison and Susan, 1972. The green revolution. *Environment, 14*:32–39.

chapter four

How Much Can You Take?

And because I love you
I'll give it one more try
To tell my rainbow race
It's too soon to die.

Pete Seeger, "My Rainbow Race"

Pollution—A Persistent Problem

People and pollution go together. It is not that the human species is necessarily more dirty than other animals, but it shares with some other species a tendency to congregate, and to collect materials that in time become "solid wastes" or rubbish. Anthropologists identify the home sites of primitive peoples by their garbage dumps—shell mounds, and the like. Some of these, when new, ripe, and fully utilized, must have been stinking indeed. However, primitive peoples, at most times, had adequate space to roam in and the freedom to pick up and move their camp sites or villages when conditions became unbearable. All of their waste materials were organic or derived from the earth, and could in time be incorporated in it once more.

79

Pollution as a problem came with city living. Whenever people become crowded into an area the disposal of their organic wastes becomes difficult. In some early cities it is likely that sewage was carried to the farms for use as fertilizer, but this was not a universal practice. Rome was one of the first cities to develop a system of water disposal of human wastes, along with indoor plumbing. But its major sewer, the Cloaca Maxima, did not serve all of the people and sanitary conditions in the city were far from satisfactory (Mumford, 1961).

The growth of civilization and advanced technology, with the industrial revoution, served initially to add new dimensions to urban pollution problems. The miserable conditions of life in nineteenth century urban England, for example, have been described by Frederick Engels (1892), Sir Arthur Bryant (1968), and others. A quotation from William Morris, writing in 1887, is only matched in some of the environmental writing of today (Allaby, 1973).

"Shall I tell you what luxury has done for you in modern Europe? It has covered the merry green fields with the hovels of slaves, and blighted the flowers and trees with poisonous gases, and turned the rivers into sewers; till over many parts of Britain the common people have forgotten what a field or flower is like, and their idea of beauty is a gas-poisoned gin-palace, or a tawdry theatre. And civilisation thinks that is all right, and doesn't heed it. . . ."

It follows that pollution is not a new problem, but one that mankind has grappled with for many years. It is equally true that pollution is not a unique contribution or concern of the economically developed nations of the earth, but is a problem that plagues the Third World as well. Thus, writing about Peru, Jon Tinker (1974) has provided this account of a mining town associated with the Cerro de Pasco mines.

"La Oroya is even more unlovely, a dreary huddle of barracks and slums, where human turds litter the backstreets, and children share with the dogs the task of picking over the roadside garbage. Dominating everything else is the smelter chimney whose leaded sulphurous fumes fall heavily over the town. La Oroya lies in a narrow valley, whose sides are well above the stack outlet, so its gases are often trapped in the immediate vicinity. The sulphur dioxide is intense enough to have *completely* denuded the surrounding hills of all vegetation, a condition which maintains up to 8 km downwind.

"The effects on the inhabitant's health have never been evaluated, but it is hard to believe they are not substantial. The smell is indescribable. There is dust everywhere, laced with lead to add extra flavour. There is the sweet, back-of-the-throat aroma of sulphur dioxide, plus the sharp tang of ammonia. . . . 20 km and more away the grass contains so much lead that the sheep's wool becomes coarse, crinkly and unsaleable if they spend more than a couple of months on contaminated pasture."

The mines of Peru have been owned by the Cerro de Pasco Corporation, mostly of United States ownership, and have been nationalized only in 1973. This then is an example of America's contribution to Peruvian welfare. It also should be noted that the Peruvian government did not act to force the company to correct this problem.

Anyone who travels much in Third World countries will be familiar with similar situations, since most commonly the people who are most seriously affected by pollution have little political power, and often no knowledge that it is possible to change the situation without sacrificing their livelihood. Furthermore there has been strong opposition by Third World politicians, most notably at the United Nations Conference on the Human Environment in 1972, to any program for pollution control, unless the cost of such control be borne by the wealthier nations of the world.

Pollution may be defined as the accumulation of substances, or forms of energy, in the environment in quantities, or at rates of flow, which exceed the capacity of ecosystems to either neutralize or disperse them to harmless levels. Pollutants are not necessarily harmful in themselves. Thus human feces can be regarded either as a pollutant or as a useful fertilizer. If distributed properly on agricultural soils they enter into biogeochemical cycles and enrich crop yields. However, when accumulated in areas where numbers of people live, they become obnoxious pollutants and a source of disease. Carbon dioxide is a harmless gas, but it if accumulates to the exclusion of oxygen, it becomes a pollutant, or if too great an amount is present in the atmosphere, it becomes an agent of climate change. Some pollutants, however, are harmful even in small quantities.

Nuclear Radiation and Pesticides

The hell-metal, plutonium, was not found on earth until it was produced by mankind in the rush to create an atomic bomb. Any particle is harmful to life. It is generally known that the breakdown of any radioactive material, with the consequent emission of high-energy radiation, is harmful to living organisms in the vicinity. Yet exposure to radiation is unavoidable, both because of the presence of radioactive materials in the earth's crust, and in the oceans, but also because cosmic radiation from space penetrates the earth's atmosphere. This so-called "background" radiation, from all sources, averages 88 millirems per year. By contrast a single particle of plutonium oxide, lodged in the lungs, will expose nearby tissues to 4000 rems per year (*New Scientist,* 1974).

(A rem, or roentgen equivalent man, is a measure of radiation absorbed by the human body. One rem is one roentgen absorbed by a human, and is the equivalent of 100 ergs of energy per gram of tissue. A millirem is one thousandth of a rem.)

Arguments continue to rage over what can be considered a "maximum permissible" degree of exposure to radiation. For workers in the nuclear industry this maximum permissible exposure is set at 15 rems per year. This does not mean that 15 rems per year will do no harm, but only that some expert group has decided that the statistical probability of being harmed in any serious way by such a level of exposure is "slight." In fact, if we were not determined to develop nuclear weapons and nuclear power there would be no reason for any person to be exposed to more than the normal background radiation, except when the use of medical x-rays is required.

Arguments also go on over the quantities of pesticides to which people may be safely exposed. One supporter of DDT has attempted to prove it harmless by swallowing spoonfuls of it, however in laboratory experiments it has been found that 250 milligrams per kilogram of water will kill half of a population of white rats forced to ingest this solution, and 0.005 milligrams per liter of water will kill 50 percent of the fish in that water. DDT is recognized, however, as one of the least toxic, to mammals, of the organochlorine pesticides. By contrast endrin is one of the most toxic and 12 milligrams per kilogram will kill half the white rats. Nobody argues that the organophosphate pesticide parathion is not toxic (8 milligrams per kilogram) since many farm workers, particularly in developing countries, have died from exposure to parathion (Shea, 1969).

It is generally agreed that no toxic heavy metals should be ingested or inhaled by people. Lead, arsenic, mercury, cadmium, chromium, and nickel are poisonous as are other, less common metals. However, they are present in the environment naturally and some consumption is unavoidable. Human activities, such as the burning of leaded gasoline, increase the quantities in the environment and the likelihood of serious poisoning. How much should we dare to tolerate in order to gain such benefits as quieter automobile engines?

Pollution is no simple problem, and pollution control cannot be aimed, sensibly, at the removal of all harmful substances or energy from the environment. We cannot even aim, realistically, at the restoration of the environment to preindustrial levels of pollution unless we are prepared to give up the products of industrial technology. We can, however, strive toward an environment in which levels of pollution create no unreasonable risk to human health, and at which the functioning of natural ecosystems is not impaired. However, this goal is seldom to be gained by regarding pollution as a separate thing, but instead by examining and remodeling the total system that causes an output of pollutants.

To focus attention on some specific pollution problems and to seek answers to them, it is worthwhile to begin with chemical pesticides, notably the broad-spectrum, organochlorine insecticides, both because these have been well studied, and because they remain a center of controversy. The term "broad spectrum" refers to the fact that these insecticides do not just kill the target insect toward which they are directed, but a broad spectrum of life, including amphibians, reptiles, fish, birds, and at various levels of concentration, mammals. The term "biocide" is therefore applied to them. As noted earlier, they are persistent in the environment, meaning that they are not rapidly broken down by most physical or biological processes that occur in the biosphere. Because of their toxicity and persistence these chemicals have the capacity for accumulating in food chains and interfering with the functioning of ecosystems to a major degree. They create (as noted in Chapter Two) "superpests," which have become resistant to the effects of pesticides; insect plagues, through destruction of normal predators on plant-eating insects; and destruction of bird life. Nevertheless, they are often initially helpful in controlling insects, and through using various kinds and combinations of these chemicals, some degree of control can be maintained for several years. Consequently they continue to be used for purposes of public health and for the protection of farm crops.

The methods by which insecticides are dispersed vary considerably. The greatest environmental damage is done by aerial spraying. Thus, in Java, in an effort to improve rice yields, DDT was sprayed over the rice paddies. This resulted in the death of fish that lived in the paddies, and the loss of an important source of protein for the peasants who were supposedly to be benefited. It did little harm, however, to the wealthy land-holders, who were interested in a cash crop of rice and not in the production of fish (Franke, 1974). Comparatively little environmental damage is done, by contrast, through the hand application of DDT inside houses as a means for controlling malaria mosquitoes—although there are good arguments against this practice also. (Farvar and Milton, 1972).

At present, DDT continues to be used in the control of malaria mosquitoes, and various other disease-bearing insects in the tropical world. Reasons in favor of its continuing use have been sufficiently compelling, because of the direct saving of human lives through the control of disease, that it seems unlikely that its use will be abandoned by public health authorities until such time as an equally cheap and effective, but less environmentally harmful, substitute can be found. Pesticide-resistant malaria mosquitoes have developed in some areas, but this phenomenon does not appear to be as frequent as the development of pesticide resistance in insects that attack farm crops.

Unfortunately, the use of organochlorine insecticides has become part and parcel of Green Revolution agriculture, and this approach to enhancing crop yields is still most widely advocated for developing countries. Disadvantages of this approach have been discussed in chapter three, related particularly to the question of energy use in farm machinery, pesticide, and fertilizer production. Nevertheless, those who advocate abandonment of the widespread use of pesticides, and indeed of this entire chemical-mechanical approach to crop production, are accused of callousness and indifference to human suffering. Without this approach, it is stated, crop yields will fall and people will suffer. With this approach, however, we seem to be heading toward an eventual global collapse of agriculture, if for no other reason than the inability to maintain a system that requires more energy calories in agricultural input than are obtained in output. Furthermore the damage done to soil organisms, as well as to the functioning of the entire agricultural ecosystem will make recovery, after such a collapse, more difficult.

To make this entire program seem even more insane it has been pointed out by Nicholas Gould (1974) that "productivity per acre is in inverse proportion to productivity per man." The Green Revolution agriculture results in a greatly enhanced productivity per man, by eliminating most human labor on farms and replacing it with fossil-fuel energy inputs. However, intensive hand care per acre would produce greater yields, without a high energy drain. Again, Gould has pointed out that when, in the United Kingdom, farming lands are replaced by housing tracts, food production from the land actually increases. The reason is the intensive hand care devoted to raising crops on small kitchen gardens. Traditional peasant agriculture, similarly, has produced an energy surplus, since the people and farm animals who work the land are fed from the land, use few inputs of outside energy, and nevertheless, when successful, produce food for sale or exchange.

To examine another way in which our agricultural and urban systems are out of joint and contribute in a major way to world pollution problems it is worthwhile to consider urban sewage and agricultural fertilization.

Sewage and Fertilizer

One of the most interesting accounts of an urban sewage problem is available oddly enough, in *Rolling Stone,* March 14, 1974. In an article entitled *It'll knock 'em dead on Broadway,* Michael Rogers has described the New York sewage disposal situation. New York City has expended considerable effort in the construction of sewage treatment plants. In these, raw sewage is run through a system of aeration and settling that separates out the solids. In the better plants clean water is produced and even some methane gas that is used to operate the plant itself. However the residue of treated solids is sewage sludge, concentrated human feces plus other materials. Unable to find an economical way of disposing of this material on land (it amounts to nearly 5 million cubic yards of concentrated sewage), New York has hauled it in barges approximately 11 miles into the Atlantic and dumped it where, hopefully, it would work its way down the submarine canyon of the Hudson River and be dispersed through the ocean. In Rogers' words:

"The process is politely known as sludge-dumping, and New York City is, without contest, the sludge-dumping capital of the US. With 40 years of experience and a five-barge fleet making six ocean forays every day of the week, New York's chances of retaining the title look excellent. Only a single difficulty may yet interfere: Those four decades of gooey black concentrated sewage lying 100 feet below the choppy surface of the Atlantic—a vile, putrid, virus-infested blob estimated to cover 15-square miles—may have already begun a long, slow and unstoppable migration across the sandy sea-floor, back, unerringly, toward the beaches of its origin.

"If it arrives on the beaches, it will likely have the appearance of wet black talcum powder, rife with fecal bacteria, an assortment of heavy metals—mercury, lead, zinc, copper, chromium—and a textbook spectrum of viruses from hepatitis and encephalitis to polio and meningitis."

It is not known as yet why this backward creep of the sludge is taking place, since there is much to be learned about the oceanography of the area. It is not known whether the sludge mass, now moving at approximately one mile a year, will continue until it hits the beaches. It is known that the sludge area is extremely toxic to life, and it is probable that the situation will get worse until such time as New York City finds a different way of handling its sewage. If it does hit the beaches, New Yorkers will have to find some other place to cool off on warm, summer days, or risk the consequences.

At the other extreme of this technological spectrum are the nation's forests, farms, and pasture lands all capable of being benefited by organic fertilizer. Human sewage is a source of organic fertilizer, as are animal and plant wastes, generally. However, the nation's farms make use of inorganic fertilizer—mixtures of nitrogen, phosphates, and potassium mined or manufactured at great cost of energy. Nitrogen fertilizers are derived, for the most part, from natural gas, which is in equally short supply with petroleum, and their production requires power from fossil-fuel (or nuclear) plants. Furthermore, Barry Commoner (1972) and others have described the dangers and problems involved in excessive use of inorganic nitrate fertilizers. Not only are excess nitrates, remaining in food, capable of being transformed under certain conditions into nitrites and nitrosamines, which can be toxic, but they cause much more widespread damage when they drain off farm lands and enter streams and lakes.

Lake Erie, which receives the excess fertilizer draining off a great area of midwestern farm lands, as well as a variety of urban wastes, has been held up as an example of a dying lake. Its sickness is known as *eutrophication,* a process resulting from excessive fertilization of water bodies. When fertilizers are present in quantities that are in excess of the capacity of normally occurring food chains to cycle them, conditions become favorable for the rapid growth of species able to respond to these "boom" conditions. There will be blooms of green or blue-green algae, filling the surface waters of the lake with plant plankton, causing profuse growth of rooted plants on the lake margins, and resulting in the development of floating mats of vegetation. When this material finally sinks and decomposes in the deeper waters and lake bottoms, oxygen is exhausted. Under the anaerobic conditions that develop only those organisms capable of living without oxygen can exist, and these in turn give off such metabolic products as hydrogen sulfide and methane, making the waters still less suitable to life. The end result, for the lake bottom, is a black, gooey sludge similar to what results from sewage dumping off New York.

Howard Odum (1973) has stated that "Environmental technology which duplicates the work available from the ecological sector is an economic handicap." In American society we have examined two extremes of this: one the elaborate processing and hauling of sewage for dumping in the ocean, the other the energy-consuming production of excess amounts of inorganic fertilizer to be used on farms in place of organic wastes. Both represent, in the long run, economic handicaps.

The reasons for the use of inorganic fertilizers in place of manure on farms are several. Manufactured fertilizers have been cheap until recently, since petroleum was cheap. They are relatively easy to handle and spread by mechanical means. The new hybrid grains and other modern varieties of crop plants are specifically bred for their ability to respond quickly to these fertilizers. Draught livestock have been replaced by tractors, which produce no manure, and, in consequence, sources of abundant organic fertilizer are often somewhat distant from the farms that might use it.

The answer is not simply to haul raw sewage from the cities out to the farms. Among other things this can create serious health problems, as is witnessed in those Asian regions where this is practiced, and where in consequence diseases carried by bacteria, protozoa, or viruses in human wastes are widespread. In Africa, for example, one of the most widespread and debilitating diseases is bilharzia, a form of schistosomiasis. The schistosome travels in its life cycle from the human urinary tract to water, to an aquatic snail, back to water and then through the skin of any human whom it encounters in the water (Van der Schalie, 1972). If human urine could be kept out of the water, the cycle would be broken. Instead, the disease causes sickness and early death for millions of African people.

Assuming that the health problems could be overcome, and they can, it would take a lot of freight cars to haul 5 million cubic yards of New York City sewage sludge to pass out among unwilling farmers. The answer is not easy to find. It may be that huge urban agglomerations, such as New York City, as presently constituted are ecologically unviable. But they are with us, and for the present at least we must try to live with them, and seek what may be interim solutions. In fact, major European cities long ago found such solutions. In Paris and Berlin municipal waste water is pumped to sewage farms outside the city. These have been in operation since 1850 and are highly productive. It is important, however, to keep industrial wastes that may contain heavy metals or other toxic substances separate from organic sewage, where this will be used directly on farms. Farm soils seem to be adequate to cope with sewage bacteria, so that water percolating through these soils to a depth of 3 feet has been found to be free from coliform bacteria. Plans have been developed by the Army Corps of Engineers to pump municipal waste water from Chicago to a large sewer farm 25 miles south of the city (Allen, 1973).

The city of Milwaukee converts its sewage sludge into "Milorganite," a dried, odorless, disease-free substance that is sold as fertilizer to gardeners, if not yet extensively to farmers. Such a process consumes energy. However, all of the energy can be generated by the sewage itself. Thus, in Britain, two thirds of the 5000 sewage treatment plants produce their own methane, which is used to operate all of their processing machinery. The Southend and Mogden plants produce excess methane, which is sold as heating gas. New methods of generating methane, using pulverised organic additives, greatly enhance production, with the result that 13 cubic feet of methane can be produced from every pound of raw material. The dried and purified sludge is then available as fertilizer (*New Scientist,* 1974).

At the Seabrook Farms in Maryland, water-borne organic wastes have been sprayed into forest areas of sandy soil where they have enhanced forest growth and improved the soil conditions. At Pennsylvania State College considerable research has gone into the disposal of water-borne sewage both on farm lands, and during the winter on forest and scrub land. Good results have been obtained on both types of areas (Allen, 1973; Dasmann, 1973).

However, it seems likely that central collection, treatment, and disposal of urban sewage is not likely to prove to be the most economical nor ecologically sound method for handling organic wastes. Instead, a smaller scale and decentralized approach may have greater merit. It is possible to build urban structures that are virtually self contained. These can generate their own electrical power through wind generators or solar cells, or can produce methane for heating by the anaerobic breakdown of organic wastes. They could be built to handle this breakdown of organic materials without the need for excessive quantities of water such as are now required in city sewage systems. Loss of power and heat in transmission would be avoided in such self-contained structures. Alternatively, however, it may prove more economically attractive to carry out these functions on a neighborhood scale, with local, centralized collecting systems that provide for the recycling of water.

Andrew MacKillop (1973) has stressed the importance of localized power plants in energy conservation, as compared to the present centralized power stations. These latter distribute electricity over power-wasting and space-consuming electrical grids. In the conventional British electric power system the efficiency of electrical generation is no more than 27 percent. The balance of energy in the original fuel is lost as heat. In a central power plant there is an output of waste heat of 1300 megawatts for every 1000 megawatts of electricity generated, when fossil fuels are used. In nuclear plants the waste heat amounts to 2100 megawatts per thousand megawatts of electricity. In most central power plants this heat cannot be used locally, but is discharged into rivers, lakes, or coastal waters in the form of hot water, or into the atmosphere when the heated water is passed through cooling towers. Such disposal creates problems of thermal pollution and is a waste of useful energy.

In a local power-generating plant operating at Vasteras, Sweden, the heat produced is used for local district heating, so that the output of the plant is nearly 85 percent efficient. For every 1650 MW of fuel input, there is an output of 900 MW of useful heat, and 500 MW of electricity. Pollution and waste are thus drastically reduced. A plant being constructed in Nottingham, England, will use 200,000 tons of rubbish for every 20,000 tons of coal. This mixture will produce 1.5 MW of electricity, and 33 MW of heat for each of 7000 homes in the district. Metals and ash will be salvaged from the rubbish and the plant will have little polluting effect.

It is impossible, of course, to immediately convert our excessively wasteful and highly polluting urban and agricultural systems to low-waste, conservation-oriented systems with low outputs of pollutants. However, it is essential to realize now the essential insanity of our existing ways of handling problems of both pollution and production, and to move as rapidly as possible to methods that can be sustained over the long run. We can only accomplish this, without total breakdown, if we move from energy-wasting and pollution-producing systems to low-energy input, low-pollution systems during the period while we still have reasonably abundant supplies of fossil-fuel energy. This does not leave us much longer to stall around.

Oil Pollution

In 1967 the general public was first made aware of the dangers of ocean pollution by oil when the giant oil tanker, the Torrey Canyon, broke up on a reef off the southwest coast of Great Britain. Millions of gallons of crude oil moved onto England's beaches and across the channel to hit the shores of France. A massive cleanup campaign took place, and great effort went into ways and means of controlling oil spills. Serious biological damage was done to marine life as well as to recreational facilities. In 1969 a different sort of danger from marine pollution was revealed when an oil well being drilled beneath the Santa Barbara Channel in California caused a leak to occur in the roof of the oil-bearing strata. Oil bubbled to the surface and spread in an ever-growing slick to wash up on Santa Barbara's beaches, destroy thousands of sea birds, and wipe out entire intertidal biotic communities (Breeden, 1971).

During subsequent years one disaster followed another, and it was revealed that in addition to the oceanic pollution resulting from accidental oil spills and blowouts from wells, there was considerable deliberate pollution caused by oil tankers flushing out their holds while at sea, as well as a growing amount of pollution resulting from the use of gasoline or other fuels in shipping and pleasure boats. In a voyage across the South Atlantic, anthropologist Thor Heyerdahl reported encountering floating petroleum or petroleum tar throughout his voyage in the papyrus raft *Ra*. Similar accounts have since come in from other supposedly remote ocean areas. Oil pollution of the oceans has become a global phenomenon, although evidence of its full effect on marine life remains inadequate.

The Study of Critical Environmental Problems (SCEP) (1970), sponsored by the Massachusetts Institute of Technology, reported that additions of petroleum to the ocean through accidental spills amounted to only 10 percent of the total oil added to the waters of the globe. The rest, 90 percent was found to come in normal operations of ships, refineries, petrochemical plants, submarine oil wells, the disposal of waste lubricants, and other automotive and industrial oils, and fallout of airborne hydrocarbons emitted by automobiles and industries. The oil in the oceans was found to represent at least 0.1 percent of total crude oil production, and perhaps as much as 0.5 percent, and equalled at least 2.1 million metric tons of oil. Since production was being increased, and still larger oil tankers were being built, including 800,000 ton vessels, the dangers of increased pollution were obvious.

The study noted the severe effects on marine life of certain oil spills, and the less obvious effects of others, and recognized serious dangers that could result over the long run. Oil slicks, for example, appear to concentrate oil-soluble pesticides such as DDT or dieldrin, and one studied off Miami revealed 10,000 times more dieldrin in the thin surface slick than in the water immediately below. This could, of course, bring extreme danger to surface feeding marine life, including zooplankton.

In its 1973 report the federal Council on Environmental Quality (CEQ) discussed some of the findings of the National Science Foundation's International Decade of Ocean Exploration, as well as studies carried out by the National Ocean and Atmospheric Agency (NOAA). The widespread distribution of petroleum in the form of tar balls throughout the oceans and their association with dissolved chlorinated hydrocarbon pesticides as well as the equally dangerous PCB's (polychlorinated biphenyls) in high concentrations was observed. It was elsewhere noted that these tar balls seemed to attract marine organisms, perhaps for shelter, and thus increased the likelihood of their experiencing ill effects from these materials. These studies also noted widespread contamination of the ocean by plastic debris in the "form of sheets, beads, discs, and also bits of styrofoam." The CEQ further noted that approximately 1.5 million metric tons of oil enters the oceans from bilge pumping, tank cleaning, and ballast discharges each year compared to only 250,000 metric tons from vessel accidents.

The oceans remain no-man's waters, and except for the coastal strips claimed by nations, are subject only to international control. As noted earlier such control has been lacking, since nations are free to go their own way regardless of what treaties they may, or may not, sign. Essentially we depend on the good will or good behavior of oil companies and other vessel operators, and to date neither the will nor the behavior has been very good. Effective control would depend on nations agreeing to give some international body effective authority to enforce the law and the police apparatus with which to carry it out. In 1974, anticipating the United Nations Law of the Sea Conference, any such international agreement seems unlikely.

In 1974, responsibility for international control over oil pollution rests with IMCO, the Inter-Governmental Maritime Consultative Organization of the United Nations. IMCO has concentrated its efforts toward better design of oil tankers, to reduce the need for tank flushing, and reduce the danger of complete loss of oil resulting from collisions. It has further attempted to extend the width of coastal strips in which all discharge of oil is to be prohibited (CEQ, 1973).

Regrettably, in 1974, the "oil crisis" has caused nations to put aside environmental standards and to further emphasize the development of offshore oil deposits such as those along the coast of Southern California, along the Gulf Coast of Florida, in the waters of South Vietnam, in the Arctic Ocean, the North Sea, and elsewhere. Such development makes it certain that there will be further disasters of the type that afflicted the Santa Barbara Channel.

It is perhaps fortunate for the life of the world's oceans, that petroleum supplies are running out. The danger seems to lie in frantic efforts on the part of nations to "get their share" from the last reserves. One cannot predict whether marine life can survive another 30 years of irresponsible exploitation of petroleum resources.

PCB's

In 1970 the Study of Critical Environmental Problems noted that "Man produces more than a million different kinds of products both as waste and as useful products that eventually end up as waste." Some of these are known to be lethal or highly toxic to living organisms. Others are believed harmless. In between is a wide range of materials with varying degrees of toxicity measured over the short or the long term. Long term effects of low-level doses of various toxic materials are not known, since it can take a generation or more for their effects to become obvious. Furthermore, for many of the chemicals now being produced and released into the biosphere neither the short nor long term effects are known. Thus the PCB's (polychlorinated biphenyls) are extremely complicated organic chemicals that may occur in 102 or more different combinations. They were first described in 1881, and first manufactured successfully in 1930 (Peakall and Lincer, 1970). It was not until 1969, however, when they were found in association with a massive "die-off" of British sea birds that their prevalence in the environment, and the hazards that they represented were realized. Since then they have been found virtually everywhere and associated with many forms of wildlife mortality (Shea, 1973). They have been used in a variety of industrial products, including paint, but since their hazards have been revealed their use in the United States has been restricted. The Council on Environmental Quality reported in 1973; "The major U.S. producer of PCB's, the Monsanto Company, voluntarily limited sales of these chemicals to use in capacitators and transformers (from which it was considered unlikely that they would contaminate the environment). But there is no legal authority to prevent other manufacturers, either domestic or foreign, from supplying PCB's for any use."

The Council further noted the international agreement in 1973 on the part of the Organization for Economic Cooperation and Development (OECD) to limit the use of PCB's to a rather wide range of industrial purposes. However, it is pointed out that "This is the first international agreement limiting the use of an industrial chemical for environmental reasons." As noted above, PCB's are now found throughout the marine environment.

Automobiles and Air

Among the various forms of madness, in the name of progress, in which the United States has indulged certainly one of the most extreme has been that associated with the automobile industry. This and the related highway-building program have led to many forms of environmental destruction, a massive waste of energy resources, and a great increase in the pollution of the air.

The last 30 years have seen the decline of the American railroad system to the point where passenger transportation between most cities has ceased to exist, and in those areas in which it survives is inadequate. Railroad companies have gone bankrupt. City-electric rail systems have virtually all disappeared, along with interurban electric-train networks. Water borne transport has undergone a similar decline. In place of these systems, the country has been blanketed with a dense network of paved highways intended to carry a growing number of private automobiles and transport trucks. Air travel has extensively replaced both rail and sea transport.

What has happened has been the replacement of energy-efficient, low-pollution transport with energy-inefficient, high-pollution transport. To accomplish this the automobile industry, the oil companies, the federal government, state governments, and local governments have worked together to bring the nation to a nonviable condition. One could readily suspect a conspiracy in which private profit was placed above public good at public cost. But the conspirators would include the majority of the American people.

Although the automobile industry has always been supported by public subsidy, since the public pays for the construction of the roads on which automobiles must run, the extent of this subsidy didn't reach major proportions until the passage by Congress in 1956 of the Federal-Aid Highway Act. This provided a tax on gasoline from which funds were placed in a Highway Trust Fund. This fund was then used to provide 90 percent of the cost of construction of the interstate highway network. Between 1956 and 1970 over 43 billion dollars were spent to built 31,900 miles of interstate freeways (Kopper, 1971). During the same period less than 1 billion dollars went to bolster up the failing railroad system (Entwistle, 1973). Interstate highways were allowed precedence over most other forms of land use, and have completely shattered urban networks, run through park and wilderness areas, paved over choice farmland and destroyed invaluable wetlands. As a result of this emphasis on the highway and the automobile, most Americans have become helplessly dependent on their automobiles and many cannot survive, in the areas where they must live, without the use of their cars. Although it cannot be denied that Americans want automobiles and exhibit a great love for their favorite vehicles, it is the dependence on them that is frightening. Because of this dependence, a fuel shortage, such as was provided for Americans by the government and oil companies in 1973-1974 caused frantic panic.

In 1973 automobiles consumed 29 percent of all the petroleum used in the country. In the same year the auto industry consumed 21 percent of the steel, 10 percent of aluminum, 55 percent of lead, 14 percent of nickel, 37 percent of zinc, and 69 percent of the natural rubber consumed in the United States. In addition, transportation produced 42 percent of the air pollution emissions in the United States, and in many cities helped to bring about an air pollution crisis (CEQ, 1970; Entwistle, 1973).

The automobile is powered by an internal-combustion engine that consumes gasoline or diesel fuel. This happens to be an inefficient engine that only partially burns the fuel that passes through the cylinders. If gasoline were burned completely, as it is in certain external combustion or steam engines, the end products would be carbon dioxide and water and little harm to the environment would result. Instead automobile exhaust pipes give off carbon monoxide, a deadly gas, and are responsible for 64 percent of the carbon monoxide that enters the nation's atmosphere each year. In addition they give off a variety of hydrocarbons and nitrogen oxides (CEQ, 1970; Kopper, 1971).

Automobile exhaust fumes are dangerous enough in themselves. However, when they are acted on by sunlight in the atmosphere they become more dangerous. Some of the hydrocarbons and nitrogen oxides give off free oxygen atoms that combine to form ozone (O_3), a potentially lethal gas, and one that in small amounts is irritating to people and damaging to plant crops. Other free oxygen atoms join with other hydrocarbons to form peroxyacetyl nitrates (PANs) that cause irritation to the eyes and respiratory system, and are particularly damaging to plants. In addition a variety of other irritating or damaging chemicals are formed, which altogether produce the atmospheric condition known as smog (CEQ, 1970; Kopper, 1971).

Smog first became famous in Los Angeles, where a combination of plentiful sunlight, frequent temperature inversions (which hold fumes near the ground), and a near total dependence on automobiles for transportation, caused the air to turn brown, the scenery to disappear, vegetation to be damaged, and people to be left gasping. The relation between automobile exhaust emissions and the presence of smog was first discovered by Dr. A. J. Haagen-Smit of the California Institute of Technology in Pasadena. Because of its severe air pollution problem, Los Angeles was one of the first cities to take vigorous action to control this form of pollution, and California led the nation in passing laws to control automobile exhaust emissions. Later, when it was recognized that the problem was not confined to California, but was nationwide, the federal government acted to demand that automobile manufacturers install pollution control devices that would greatly reduce the output of carbon monoxide, hydrocarbons, and nitrogen oxides. All of these efforts have helped to alleviate, but not yet solve the problem (CEQ, 1970).

The answer to air pollution problems, resulting from automotive transport, is the same as the answer to the overconsumption of scarce fuels by the same vehicles. One of the first steps is restoration of an efficient public transportation, to replace and improve on the ones that we have either destroyed or allowed to fall apart. The federal government and local governments have belatedly started a program to accomplish this. The San Francisco Bay Area, which once had an efficient interurban electric train system, now has, at great cost, a replacement known as BART, the Bay Area Rapid Transit system (Kopper, 1971). The railroads are slowly being rejuvenated and rapid passenger service is being established between major cities. However, public transport alone will not solve pollution problems nor will it satisfy the public, which for some time to come will both need and want private cars of some sort. Efficient, low-pollution, motors using renewable or inexhaustible resources have been built. These include motors powered by various alcohols, such as ethanol or methanol, and those powered by methane gas, hydrogen, and other fuels. For as long as we do use petroleum for fuel, engines need be built that will use it efficiently and, in consequence, produce little or no air pollution. Many such engines have been designed but not seriously developed.

The inertia of the American economic, social, and political system has always guaranteed that we will go on doing the wrong thing, with greater expenditure of effort, long after it has been revealed to be wrong. No doubt for a while, yet we will continue to build superhighways and inefficient, polluting vehicles to run on them. But barring some technological breakthrough that will permit us to destroy virtually everything worthwhile in our environment, it appears that in the field of transportation and its related air pollution we will be forced to adopt sanity.

References

Allaby, Michael, 1973. Nothing new. *Ecologist, 3*: 436–437.

Allen, Jonathan, 1973. Sewage farming. *Environment, 15*: 36–41.

Breeden, Robert L., ed., 1971. *As we live and breathe.* National Geographic Society, Washington.

Bryant, Sir Arthur, 1968. *Set in a silver sea.* Doubleday, New York.

Commoner, Barry, 1972. Remarks. *The careless technology.* Natural History Press, New York, pp. 657–658.

Council on Environmental Quality (CEQ), 1970. *Environmental quality.* Superintendent of Documents, Washington.

Dasmann, R. F., 1972. *Environmental conservation.* 3rd ed., John Wiley, New York.

Engels, Frederick, 1892. *The condition of the working class in England.* (1969 ed.) Panther Books, London.

Entwistle, Robert, 1973. The crisis we won't face squarely. *Sierra Club Bull., 58*: 9–12, 32.

Farvar, M. Taghi, and J. P. Milton, 1972. *The careless technology.* Natural History Press, New York.

Franke, Richard, 1974. Miracle seeds and shattered dreams in Java. *Natural History, 83*: 10–18, 84–88.

Gould, Nicholas, 1974. England's Green Revolution. *Ecologist, 4*: 58–60.

Hills, Lawrence D., 1972. Sanitation for conservation. *Ecologist, 2*: 24–26.

Kopper, Philip, 1971. Transportation. Nation on the go. *As we live and breathe,* pp. 118–141, National Geographic Society, Washington.

MacKillop, Andrew, 1973. Unravel the grid! *Ecologist, 3*: 412–418.

Mumford, Lewis, 1961. *The city in history.* Harcourt, Brace, World, New York.

New Scientist, 1974. Methane, the most natural gas. *New Scientist, 61*: 407.

———, 1974. Plutonium cancer warning spells trouble for breeders. *New Scientist, 61*:542.

Odum, Howard T., 1973. Energy, ecology, and economics. *Ambio, 2*: 220–227.

Peakall, David B. and J. L. Lincer, 1970. Polychlorinated biphenyls. *Bioscience, 20*: 958–963.

Rogers, Michael, 1974. It'll knock 'em dead on Broadway. *Rolling Stone,* 14 March.

Study of Critical Environmental Problems (SCEP), 1970. *Man's impact on the global environment.* Massachusetts Institute of Technology, Cambridge.

Shea, Kevin, 1969. Name your poison. *Environment, 11*:30.

——, 1973. PCB. *Environment, 15*: 25–28.

Tinker, Jon, 1974. Protection and pollution in Peru. *New Scientist, 61*:881.

Van der Schalie, Henry, 1972. World Health Organization Project Egypt 10: A case history of a schistosomiasis control project. *The careless technology*, pp. 116–136. Natural History Press, New York.

chapter five

Nobody Is at the Wheel

"Free election of masters does not abolish the masters or the slaves."

Herbert Marcuse, *One dimensional man*

A Question of Truth

At this point, having considered some of the various forms of madness that seem to characterize technological civilization, it is time to examine that civilization itself—or at least some of its characteristics. We need consider the future of the world as controlled by the needs of a technocracy—a society organized around the imperatives of high technology. We need consider whether the technological civilization of today is viable, and whether or not it can provide the means of existence and the quality of living that all of us wish to enjoy. We need consider also, alternatives to the present organization of society if in our belief it is going in the wrong direction, or will fail to provide for the survival and well being of humanity. Based on the information we can obtain, we need, each of us, to decide how we are going to live, in what life style, and what we will do to change the direction of the total society.

Almost immediately we discover that the truth is hard to find. We encounter the predictions of the technological optimists, who brush aside the obvious difficulties of the present and speak cheerfully about providing for 7 billion people in the year 2000 and 15 billion soon after that—at the same time others are calling attention to our failure to meet the needs of even half of today's population. Thus the Greek city planner and futurist, C. A. Doxiadis (1970) foresees an inevitable trend toward increasing urbanization of the world. In place of the giant urban agglomerations of today, megalopolis, he sees the development of *ecumenopolis,* a great, interconnected world city within which, by the end of the next century, at least 20 billion people will live. Somehow, science and technology must perform the miracles that will bring the virtually unlimited energy, raw materials, and food that these 20 billion will require, but we are left in the dark about how these miracles will take place.

Alvin Toffler, writing in *Future Shock* states:

> "We cannot and must not turn off the switch of technological progress. Only romantic fools babble about returning to 'a state of nature.' A state of nature is one in which infants shrivel and die for lack of elementary medical care, in which malnutrition stultifies the brain, in which, as Hobbes reminded us, the typical life is 'poor, nasty, brutish, and short.' To turn our back on technology would be not only stupid but immoral."

One could presume from this statement that the majority of people live in a "state of nature" today in such places as Calcutta, Lima, Djakarta. Our knowledge of those who live in an actual "state of nature," if by that we mean a hunter-gatherer society, has advanced far beyond Hobbes, and we find life "poor, nasty, brutish, and short" mostly among those who have been displaced and battered by the forces of technocracy, and not among the surviving "primitives." However, Toffler is well aware of the shortcomings and problems of our existing technocracy, and has a healthy fear that the "technological dream" may not be realized, or may turn into a still worse nightmare.

I cannot present fairly the viewpoints of the optimists, since the world of the present is too grim a place. However those who wish to be cheered may seek the books of Kahn and Wiener (1967), or Buckminster Fuller (1969). A whole array of technological optimists are assembled in the book *Science and Technology in the World of the Future* edited by Arthur B. Bronwell (1970). They scare me. On the other hand, virtually all of the writings that come from the Soviet Union or China, radiate optimism, with the proviso that you first follow the Marxist-Leninist pathway (Russian or Chinese branch).

In 1971 it was my fate to be keynote speaker at a conference held in Noumea, New Caledonia, an island I had not visited before. Before the conference I was taken on a tour by boat of the southern end of the island and returned in a state of discouragement. From all indications, nickel mining was in the process of totally dismembering New Caledonia, destroying the vegetation and removing top layers of soil and rock. A giant processing and smelting plant stood in the middle of Noumea. When operating this blanketed the city with noxious smoke and fumes. I changed my speech to say at one point:

"The unique forests of New Caledonia—did they really have to be destroyed? Was the profit to be obtained from their destruction so high as to justify the consequences—the scrub-covered hills, the barren, eroding slopes. . . .

"One wonders—do the powers that be, the public and private authorities, here and in France, really plan to destroy this island completely? To totally strip the surface of the land and leave nothing but devastation behind? Surely nickel or iron are not so valuable as to justify such a course. People must continue to live here. They cannot all go away. Perhaps those who make the highest profits should be required to live on the most devastated lands." (Dasmann, 1973.)

This criticism of the French company Le Nickel was taken as an attack on France. The papers next day said in essence "Swiss, Go Home!" Fortunately they did not know I was an American, or the reaction would have been stronger. The Governor-General snubbed me. Only the Pacific islanders seemed to appreciate my effort.

On Nauru, and other islands now being mined for phosphate to be used as fertilizer, there is little doubt that the plan is to totally destroy the island—or the greater part of it. Presumably the islanders can move on—to somewhere. Virtually everywhere that I have gone I find that mining, to provide the raw materials for industry and high technology takes precedence, has priority, over every other use of the land. Total destruction is permitted. Rehabilitation, if possible, rarely occurs. Everywhere an attack on mining is taken (and not without reason) as an attack on government and established society. This is the way of today's technocracy. The results of my visits to various parts of the world led me to state in Noumea that the first law of the environment for today was, "no matter how bad you think things are—the total reality is much worse."

The Growth of Technocracy

Lewis Mumford (1967, 1970), to a greater degree than anyone else, has addressed the problem of technics and technology, and in a two-volume work has reviewed the history of mankind from this perspective. In his view, large-scale machine technology (the megamachine) had its origin in the first civilizations of Egypt and Mesopotamia. The machine, however, was powered by masses of human components rather than by mechanical engines. Man himself, for the first time in his long history on earth, was made a cog or component instead of an equal partner in a human enterprise. George Leonard (1972) has commented on this idea.

"The process of formalization, bureaucratization, alienation, fragmentation—call it what you will—has gone through many stages of wax and wane, development and intensification, over the past five thousand years. But the ultimate direction is now clear. We of Civilization are the direct heirs of the first man who was moved to think of another human being as a component. We are the heirs of that component himself."

Characteristic of the megamachine was the institution of slavery, the army, a separate priesthood removed from the people, organized warfare and mass murder, and the organization of great working masses to construct massive structures for the self-glorification of those that held power. Resources, food, raw materials were drawn on to achieve these various purposes, often with the destruction of land or the depletion of its productive capacity.

The original megamachines broke down with the fall of the ancient empires. In Europe at least during the so-called Dark Ages, which were not dark at all, and the Middle Ages, society was organized on a more human scale. But the tradition of the megamachine lived on, and was to be reborn in Europe with the rise of nation states and the industrial revolution.

The industrial revolution depended initially not so much on the discovery of new power sources or the invention of efficient engines, as on the expansion of human knowledge of the world. This expansion had two components—one being spatial and resulting from the voyages of discovery and exploration, which for the first time revealed both the full extent of the world and the availability of its resources. The second was directed toward the study of the nature of things and how they operated, in other words, the rise of scientific enquiry. The rise of both science and its eventual application to technology depended in part on the religious developments of the time—particularly the increasing dualism of Christianity and Islam. This separated things of the spirit from things of the world and was in time to lead to the virtual banishment of God from the material universe—thus leaving the world free for human exploitation. Scientists and natural philosophers developed an increasingly mechanistic view of the universe, and of man himself as part of it.

The industrial revolution grew from a highly organized and effi   n medieval technology. This operated for the most part on a small, hum   scale, with the rights of its practitioners protected by the organization of craft guilds that in turn guaranteed the quality of its products. Windpower, waterpower, and horsepower in various combinations, were harnessed to carry out increasingly complex operations. The machines that were to be organized in the factories of the industrial revolution were themselves turned out by individual craftsmen who were carrying on and building from medieval tradition. In Mumford's words (1970):

"As late as the sixteenth century this dynamic and enterprising polytechnics was not only intact, but was still developing, as the wider exploration of the planet brought into Europe both natural resources and technical processes it could use to advantage. For the first time in history, the arts and technics of the world as a whole were ready to intermingle, to learn from each other, to increase the range of both their practical effectiveness and their symbolic expression. Unfortunately at that point, a change came about that fatally arrested this growth: a system of one-sided political and military domination produced its counterpart in a system of mechanization and automation that ignored the human premises upon which the older agricultural and handicraft technologies had been founded. . . . The point I am making is that if craftsmanship had not been condemned to death by starvation wages and meager profits, if it had, in fact, been protected and subsidized as so many of the new mechanical industries were in fact extravagantly subsidized, right down to jet planes and rockets today, our technology as a whole, even that of 'fine technics' would have been immensely richer—and more efficient."

The industrial revolution, with its creation of a new megamachine and the reduction once more of people to components and parts, depended on the rise of the new nation state and its professional armies—the latter to be based increasingly, after Napoleon, on universal conscription. The development of the modern nation state, although it had a long history, began to reach a peak in the eighteenth and nineteenth centuries. Each had its goddess, Britannia, Columbia, Marianne, and the like. Each could demand and extract the total loyalty of its citizens.

In America, where the old trappings of the European nation-state were initially discarded, there grew up—at least in the North and Middle West—a society based on old traditions of agricultural independence and handicraft excellence. People did not feel bound to a single occupation, but were willing and able to turn a hand to anything. Yet here, as elsewhere the old polytechnic diversity and independence was to be overwhelmed by the growth of the new technocracy, and in America it was to be carried out even more systematically and ruthlessly than in Europe. Still, there persists among perhaps a large minority of Americans, a tradition of "do-it-yourself" based on the home workshop—which, when necessary, can perform the most intricate and innovative techniques (Marsh, 1864; Mumford, 1970).

Charles A. Reich (1970) has written of the changing consciousness of the American people throughout the history of the country and describes three levels: Consciousness I (Con-I), that of the pioneer and the "rugged individualist" of the nineteenth and early twentieth century; Consciousness II (Con-II), that of today's corporate society, the consciousness of the business executive, bureaucrat, labor leader, and the like; and, finally, Consciousness III that had its origin among young people during what Alan Watts has called the "psychedelic decade" of the 1960s. I would question whether the term "consciousness" is proper, since it could be argued that most people at most times are scarcely *conscious* of anything, and that the development of consciousness in its full meaning is one of the great challenges of today. However, the distinctions made are useful.

Reich's Con-I people resemble what David Riesman (1950) has called "inner-directed people" those who guide their behavior according to the internalized rules of right and wrong, instilled by parents in childhood, or by the criteria of success/failure imbibed at the same time. Reich points out that the simple virtues "plainness, character, honesty, hard work" were admired, and morality was considered more important than intelligence. On the other side of the coin people were to be judged by their success which demanded attention to their own interests, as personally defined. Success involved getting rich and powerful and not much else. Con-I people today are those who still believe that the old nineteenth century "American dream" is relevant. They revere "free enterprise" without realizing that in the old sense it scarcely exists in a world of great industrial organizations and corporations. They favor those governments that govern least, that promise a return to low taxes, "law and order," moral rectitude, and a simple life. Spiro Agnew, before his fall, exemplified Con-I virtues in his speeches. Calvin Coolidge and Dwight Eisenhower are Con-I models for president. Disneyland is its spiritual home in the world of today.

Those who lived in the old rural and small town America, and in the nineteenth century most people did, scarcely recognized that it was no longer where the action was going on, that the power was shifting to the cities. The full impact and significance of the industrial revolution escaped them until they were submerged by it. America was changed from a rural nation to an industrial empire by the work of men who were "rugged individualists" themselves, but who gained control of coal, steel, railroads, banks, or later oil and automobiles—the Morgans, Carnegies, Vanderbilts, Harrimans, Rockefellers, and Fords. Reich states that "The true ethic that transformed America was not the ethic of piracy and rapacity standing by itself, but that of power joined to repression and order. Organization and efficiency repressed unruly, undisciplined life. It substituted the clean, spare, inhuman direction of affairs for the random, spontaneous burgeoning of life that seemed so typical of frontier America." It brought the assembly line in which each worker was a component doing one small operation over and over and neither seeing, nor being much concerned with, the finished product. The 70 and 80 hour work week, minimum pay, and the virtual absence of public services were the rule. Government existed to keep law and order, and to keep its hands off the essential work of business and industry. Monopolies grew, corporations expanded to dominate the economic life of America. Some people grew very rich indeed. Most suffered. The rapacious exploitation of minerals, fuels, land, and forests combined with a totally unrestricted right to pollute, to poison streams and foul the air.

There were those who exposed the evils of industrial America, as in the writings of Lincoln Steffens or Upton Sinclair, and there were leaders, Theodore Roosevelt, or William Jennings Bryan who sought to curb the power of corporate America. But meanwhile many Americans continued to see little difference between their own private property rights and the rights of those who controlled U. S. Steel or General Motors.

The world of Con-I declined with the Great Depression of the 1930s and received its *coup de grâce* in World War II. Government assumed increasing control and responsibility over the operation of business and industry. Labor organized and through its unions gained higher wages, the 40-hour week, social security, and a better level of public services. The old captains of industry passed on, to be replaced by a newer, blander leadership that realized that the single-minded pursuit of private profit at public cost could bring greater problems than they cared to bear. The new Con-II attitudes began to dominate society—characterized by the "organization man" or the "man in the grey flannel suit." David Riesman has characterized the people of this period as "the lonely crowd," and their orientations as "other-directed," meaning that they were finely attuned, not to their inner standards, but to the opinions and attitudes of their peer group. Such people find their place in a corporation, or a bureacracy, and almost automatically guide their activities, not so much by inner directives, but by the perceived needs of the organization, by what is "best for society."

In Charles Reich's words: "Consciousness II believes that the present American crisis can be solved by greater commitment of individuals to the public interest, more social responsibility by private business, and, above all, by more affirmative government action—regulation, planning, more of a welfare state, better and more rational administration and management." It is distrustful of the individual and his motives and puts its faith in man's ability to devise regulations and institutions to keep his own, or rather his neighbor's behavior in line. John Kennedy's inaugural speech exemplifies this consciousness: "Ask not what your country can do for you, ask what you can do for your country." A total faith in the ability of science and technology to find the answers to human problems is characteristic of this consciousness. The elitist society based on individual merit, a meritocracy, is a social goal. Just as the railroad and the assembly line can be considered as monuments to Consciousness I, the automated factory, the space rocket, and the eight-laned superhighway are monuments to this second consciousness. Suburbia is its home, exurbia is where it hopes to live. The movie *American Graffiti* is an excellent portrayal of the life of its young people.

In 1974, Reich would recognize the existence of three levels of consciousness in America, that of the young people starting in the mid-1960s and those older people who are in alliance with them—Consciousness III—and the two earlier levels. Elections for the Presidency have traditionally been battles between Consciousness I and II people. The 1972 election was unusual in that an alliance between Consciousness III and a minority of the II people led to a new orientation of the Democratic Party, and naturally enough to the overwhelming defeat of its presidential candidate.

The Nature of Technological Society

There are many different ways of describing the technological society that dominates America in the early 1970s. Galbraith (1967) calls it "The new industrial state," Reich "the American corporate state," Jacques Ellul (1964) "Technological Society," Roszak (1970) "Technocracy." All realize that it is something other than "private enterprise" doing its thing while being watched over by a benign government that has always the long-term interest of the people at heart.

In fact the separation of government and industry exists more in words than in practice. *Private* industry performs *public* work with *public* funds, whether this be the building of highways, of giant dams, war planes, guns and ammunition, or schools and colleges. Private universities are crippled in their operations when public funds for research are cut off. On the other hand much of the action at the *public* level by public employees is directed toward subsidization, regulation, or development of the private sector. The activities of the Atomic Energy Commission in relation to the private nuclear-power industry, or of the Army Corps of Engineers in relation to private contractors and power companies, are examples. The whole complex is geared toward continuing growth and progress along directions that scarcely can be modified. It can be argued that there is really nobody in charge when you reach the top—since decisions are made collectively and cannot be reversed by the person who happens to be the current general manager, executive director, chairman of the board, or even president of the United States. Planning for growth in a particular direction may involve initial consultations among representatives of many industries and branches of government. Once a decision is made contracts are let, and in turn subcontracts, people are employed and go to work, new government agencies come into existence. If it is discovered, five or ten years after the original decisions were made, that the direction is wrong—the discoverer hesitates to announce his discovery, even if he occupies a high position in industry or government. Once turned on, the megamachine rolls on, and he who stops it throws people out of work, disrupts the entire economy, and if a politician, will surely be thrown out of office.

Much of the activity of each national branch of the world technocracy is, and has long been, directed toward war. This is always disguised, in every country, as national defense. The budget of the war sector of the American economy in 1974 exceeded 80 billion dollars, a sum too large to be comprehended, but enough to' guarantee that a high percentage of the population is employed in research, development, or construction related to the various components of the war machine. During the peak years of American involvement in the Vietnam War we were spending over 20 billion dollars per year toward the destruction of Indochina—all, of course, in the name of defense. For many years it was recognized either that the war was morally wrong, or at least that it could not be won, but it was far easier to go on accelerating the destructive practices than to turn off or reverse the machine.

Productivity in the mechanical rather than the biological sense is the primary purpose of the technocracy. This is measured in terms of gross national product (GNP). Anything produced, whether useful or not, enhances GNP. Anything destroyed, if its destruction takes work and involves payrolls and machines, enhances GNP. War always boosts GNP. Production for waste has been characteristic particularly of the American technocratic society. Quality and durability are not preferred in a product, since growth of the economy is favored when it wears out and must be replaced, or when people can be persuaded to buy the latest model through the combined action of advertising and the high cost of repairs. Even major buildings are considered "temporary," since it boosts the economy to tear them down and build new "more modern" structures.

Although productivity in capitalist states is based on "private" property and produces "private" profit, the socialist model of the technocratic society, exemplified by the Soviet Union, functions in a similar way and is even less responsive to the needs or wishes of the populace. Prestige and position in the hierarchy, along with other rewards, substitute equally well for private profit.

All of the activities of the technocratic society are oriented toward the goal of "progress," which is defined in terms of continuing growth. "You can't stop progress" is the battle cry of those who identify with the system. Yet the system is wasteful and unresponsive to human needs except those that can be satisfied by material production, and is almost beyond human control. The technocratic society could continue to operate so long as energy supplies and raw materials continue to be abundant—but now, in the way it is constituted, it cannot continue to operate effectively, and unless it is modified, it will grind to a halt.

Lewis Mumford (1970) has stated that the central problem of technics "is that of creating human beings capable of understanding their own nature sufficiently to control, and when necessary to suppress, the forces and mechanisms that they have brought into existence." Instead we have forces and mechanisms that are escaping our control, and by way of warning Mumford quotes the geneticist Hermann Muller, who stresses the imperative that either one *must* learn to understand the findings of science and their application to technology or he will become ever more *useless* to the technocracy and "In this situation, his own powers of determining his fate and his very will to do so will dwindle, and the minority who rule over him will eventually find ways of doing without him." No doubt Muller meant this as a friendly warning to all of us poor cogs, but there are many who will take it as a challenge to eliminate "the minority who rule" and to dismantle the machine.

Technocracy and the Third World

One of the most disturbing features of the technocratic society has been the efforts that have been made to instill its features into the developing nations. Although the stated objectives are worthy, to remove poverty and bring living standards and food supplies up to acceptable levels, the methods used too often fail to accomplish these supposed objectives and bring in their wake both unnecessary human suffering and accelerated environmental deterioration. Nevertheless, the United Nations through all of its associated agencies, The World Bank, major private foundations such as Ford and Rockefeller, and virtually all of the Western European and North American governments continue programs of aid and technical assistance to assist Third World countries in their economic development. Admittedly the amounts of money actually deployed represent a minute fraction of the combined national defense budgets. In fact the world's 16 richest countries have given only one fifth of one percent of their gross national product in aid to developing countries, less than one tenth of the amount of money they have spent in advertising alone (Mende, 1973). However, considering the form that some of this development aid has taken, it is perhaps just as well.

In 1968 the Conservation Foundation of Washington, D.C. sponsored an international symposium, held in Airlie House, Virginia, on the ecological consequences of economic development. The results, including a series of case histories of development and its consequences, were in time published as *The Careless Technology* (1972), edited by M. Taghi Farvar and John P. Milton. Environmental consequences of such major development projects as the Aswan Dam in Egypt have included erosion of farming lands below the dam, invasion of farm lands in the Nile Delta by salt water, and their erosion by wave action, major deposition of silt within Lake Nasser behind the dam, depletion of Mediterranean fisheries, and an increased reliance on inorganic fertilizer to take the place of natural deposition of silt and humus by the Nile waters. Human consequences have included a marked increase in schistosomiasis (bilharzia) and other water-borne diseases, as well as the displacement of peoples from their traditional lands. Other major dams, Kariba Dam on the Zambesi, Volta Dam in Ghana, have had similar adverse environmental and human consequences. In all cases the dams have been successful in varying degrees in achieving their initial objectives—increased electrical power, or the provision of additional water for irrigating new lands. However, considering the massive amounts of money spent on the projects, hundreds of millions or billions of dollars, relatively little seems to filter through in the form of increased income for poor people—instead the contrast between rich and poor seems to grow more extreme.

Some projects, such as the massive deployment of pesticides, or the drilling of boreholes to increase water supply in semiarid range lands have primarily negative effects on people and the environment, although they may show some initial and temporary benefits that help accomplish local political objectives (Dasmann et al., 1973).

Richard Franke's (1974) account of the Green Revolution in Java is illustrative. Between 1967 and 1972, over 100 million dollars was spent in an effort to bring Java to a state of self-sufficiency in rice production. The goal was a crop of 15.4 million tons of rice in 1972. The production actually reached was 12.2 million tons. Wealthy land-owners, however, benefited greatly from these expenditures. Poor farmers were driven off their land. In Franke's words: "The technology advocates, the rate-of-profit theorists, the military dictators, and the large landowners are attempting to produce enough food for the people of Java. They are failing. Their optimistic plans and programs have created only increased human suffering and promise more of the same."

The concept of pouring money in from the top in developing countries and hoping it will trickle down to help the poor people appears naive at best, but considering the "rights" of nation-states and national governments, it appears the only way in which major international agencies can function. Often the true results are concealed by a comforting rise in gross national product, which causes the aid donor to believe that his efforts have been successful. One need ask, however, who benefits from the GNP increase, and who suffers.

Jimoh Omo-Fadaka (1974) states that industrialization and a high rate of growth of GNP have brought increased unemployment, poverty, and misery throughout the Third World. In Jamaica, for instance, although GNP grew at annual rates of 7.2 percent between 1950 and 1965, the actual per capita income received by the Jamaican people declined. Unemployment climbed to a high of 19 percent in urban areas, and 10 percent in rural areas—rates that would come near to inciting full-scale revolution if experienced in Europe or North America. The 140 factories that were built during this period created 9000 jobs, but 10,000 jobs were lost in the sugar industry alone by mechanization. Omo-Fadaka concludes, after examining similar data for other developing countries, that the only hope for the people must be based on low-impact technology for the support of small-scale decentralized communities. These must relate to agricultural lands that are farmed by methods that are labor intensive and require small input of imported energy. Efforts need be expended on low-cost local energy production using wind, water, and solar power. Aid should be concentrated in providing or developing low cost building materials of local origin and in establishing village industries and workshops that will encourage the maximum development of local crafts (MacKillop, 1972).

New Directions

The prescription for the developing world also seems to hold a way out for the countries now most completely dominated by technocracy. Thus Edward Goldsmith and his associates in preparing "A Blueprint for Survival" (*The Ecologist,* 1972) have primarily considered the problems of the United Kingdom. His prescription, however, is applicable elsewhere. In the preface to the "Blueprint" it is stated:

"1. An examination of the relevant information available has impressed upon us the extreme gravity of the global situation today. For, if current trends are allowed to persist, the breakdown of society and the irreversible disruption of the life-support systems on this planet, possibly by the end of the century, certainly within the lifetimes of our children, are inevitable.

"2. Governments, and ours is no exception, are either refusing to face the relevant facts, or are briefing their scientists in such a way that their seriousness is played down. Whatever the reasons, no corrective measures of any consequence are being undertaken."

The Blueprint proposes nothing less than the dismantling of the megamachine—admittedly slowly and carefully, since any sudden change could be disastrous. The prescription calls for decentralization and the development of small relatively self-sufficient communities, using ecologically sound, labor-intensive agriculture, using local and renewable energy resources, tied together by communications and public transport systems, but leaving to be done at the national, centralized level only those things that cannot be done more effectively and with less waste of energy and materials at the local level. The development of community skills and crafts could lead once more to an industry turning out durable, high quality goods that would be valued in international trade. Cessation of population growth is an immediate goal, followed by a period of slow population decline to levels that can be supported by local food production, or considering the state of the world at the time, might otherwise be considered optimum.

Reviewing the global energy picture, Howard Odum (1973) has warned:

"The terrible possibility that is before us is that there will be the continued insistence on growth with our last energies by the economic advisors that don't understand, so that there are no reserves with which to make a change, to hold order, and to cushion a period when populations must drop. Disease reduction of man and of his plant production systems could be planetary and sudden if the ratio of population to food and medical systems is pushed to the maximum at a time of falling net energy. At some point the great gaunt towers of nuclear energy installations, oil drilling, and urban cluster will stand empty in the wind for lack of enough fuel technology to keep them running."

We find ourselves faced with an imperative, which does not involve finding our place in the technocracy, but changing it. In the next few decades a new society must be built based on a durable pattern that will balance human wants with environmental necessities, and put technology, once and for all, at the service of man.

References

Bronwell, Arthur B., ed. 1970. *Science and technology in the world of the future.* Wiley-Interscience, New York.

Dasmann, R. F., John P. Milton, and Peter Freeman, 1973. *Ecological principles for economic development*. Wiley, Ltd., London.

————, 1973. Keynote address. *Regional Symposium on Conservation of Nature–reefs and lagoons*, proceedings and papers. South Pacific Commission, Noumea. pp. 130–136.

Doxiadis, C. A., 1970. Cities of the future. *Science and technology in the world of the future*. Wiley-Interscience, New York.

Ecologist, 1972. A blueprint for survival. *The Ecologist*, 2:1–43.

Ellul, Jacques, 1964. *The technological society*. Alfred Knopf. New York.

Farvar, M. Taghi and J. P. Milton, 1972. *The careless technology*. Natural History Press, New York.

Franke, Richard W., 1974. Miracle seeds and shattered dreams in Java. *Natural History*, 83:10–18, 84–88.

Fuller, Buckminster, 1969. *Operating manual for spaceship earth*. Southern Illinois University, Carbondale.

Galbraith, J. Kenneth, 1967. *The new industrial state*, Houghton Mifflin, Boston.

Kahn, Herman and Anthony J. Wiener, 1967. *The year 2000*. Macmillan, New York.

Leonard, George B., 1972. *The transformation*. Delacorte Press, New York.

MacKillop, Andrew, 1972. Low energy housing. *Ecologist*, 2:4–10.

Marsh, George Perkins, 1864. *Man and nature; or, physical geography as modified by human action*. Charles Scribner, New York.

Mende, Tibor, 1973. *From aid to re-colonization. Lessons of a failure*. Harrap, London.

Mumford, Lewis, 1967. *The myth of the machine. Technics and human development*. Harcourt, Brace & World, New York.

Mumford, Lewis, 1970. *The myth of the machine. The pentagon of power*. Harcourt Brace Jovanovich, New York.

Odum, Howard T., 1973. Energy, ecology and economics. *Ambio* (Stockholm), 11:220–227.

Omo-Fadaka, Jimoh, 1974. Industrialisation and poverty in the Third World, *The Ecologist*, 4:61–63.

Reich, Charles A., 1970. *The greening of America*. Bantam Books, New York (1971 ed.).

Riesman, David, 1950. *The lonely crowd*. Yale University Press, New Haven.

Roszak, Theodore, 1970. *The making of a counter culture*. Faber and Faber, London.

chapter six

A Place for Everything?

We are stardust
We are golden
And we've got to get ourselves
Back to the garden.

Joni Mitchell, "Woodstock"

Historical Ideas

Long before any other form of environmental problem had appeared on earth, humanity suffered serious setbacks because of failures in the use of land and its resources of water, vegetation, and soil. Today when problems of population, pollution, and technology receive particular and necessary attention, the wise and unwise use of land and water, soil, and vegetation still deserves a foremost place in our consideration. Land and water resources are basic to the long-term survival of the human race. If their productivity is maintained, humanity can survive, regardless of the fate of civilization or high technology.

One of the first techniques for land management to be developed by people was the use of fire. Back in the old stone age, the Palaeolithic, when humanity survived by hunting and food gathering, fire was used to improve hunting grounds, to capture game, and to favor wild vegetation useful for food or fiber. Where it was used it was also misused, since the management and control of fire is a difficult art. As a result the borders of forests were pushed back, whereas grasslands and open tree savannas spread at the expense of forest and woodland. Some would maintain that most of the world's savannas and grasslands developed in response to either natural or man-caused fires. Others stress the importance of soil, hydrology, and climate in the distribution of this kind of vegetation. Most agree, however, that for many of the world's savannas and grasslands, the balance between herbaceous and woody vegetation is strongly influenced by the frequency, intensity, and seasonality of fires (Sauer, 1950).

It cannot be argued that the effects of fire on the original vegetation of regions occupied by mankind were deleterious. Vegetation changed, and with it animal life, but the overall effects balanced out in favor of human survival and probably without serious effects on the wild biota.

Destructive changes in land and vegetation accompanied the domestication of plants and animals, some 11,000 or more years ago at the start of the Neolithic. Until recently the change from hunting and gathering to agriculture and pastoralism was regarded as a major step forward for mankind—permitting peace and prosperity instead of the uncertain and brutish existence of the earlier age. This view has been challenged with convincing evidence, and some now regard the development of agriculture as the factual basis for the Biblical myth of the expulsion of Adam and Eve from the Garden of Eden. Thus Waller (1971) has pointed out that "Those who have lived among hunter-gatherer societies not yet invaded by civilization report that famine is unknown and that there are no signs of nutritional diseases." Human populations are stable, and their harvesting of wild crops is based on what these animals and plants can sustain without serious depletion. The Kung Bushmen of the Kalahari are said to work an average of 20 hours a week. Along with other hunter-gatherers they have abundant time for music and dance, religious celebration, and creative art. The Bushman cave art of Africa is renowned for the feeling and understanding displayed in representation of the wild animals with which the Bushmen coexist. Lee and DeVore (1968) have pointed out that "Cultural man has been on Earth for some two million years: for over 99 per cent of this period he has lived as a hunter gatherer." They estimate that over 90 percent of all the people who have ever lived were hunter-gatherers. The persistence of this way of life, wherever it is left undisturbed, is indication of its ecological success.

Although the American Indian tribes were, for the most part, not pure hunter-gatherers, since many had considerable agricultural skills, it is worth noting that the highest population densities among North American Indians, north of Mexico and its civilizations, were supported, in California, by peoples who were hunter-gatherers. In a study of the Indians of Venezuela and Brazil, most of whom do not rely heavily on agriculture, James Neel (1970) has noted the stability of their populations, the relative immunity to disease and a generally high level of nutrition.

Whether we regard the development of agriculture as a forward step for humanity, or the beginning of madness, it led to the possibility of supporting great numbers of people and equally great numbers of their domestic animals. In the early agricultural tribes and in their villages there was no separation of man from nature. Earth was still the Great Mother to be treated with reverence and awe. Pastoralism, however, was to bring different attitudes, and it grew from the domestication of the sheep and goat, and later the cow, ass, horse, and camel, all animals adapted to graze or browse on the vegetation of the drier regions of the world. These animals could be gathered in herds and moved from place to place in search of better forage or water supplies. With pastoralism there developed, in time, the nomadic way of life, no longer dependent on fixed villages or croplands, but following instead the changes of seasons, the availability of rainfall and drinking water, and the growth of green grass. At what time in human history pastoralism and agriculture first became destructive influences can be variously argued. Certainly, however, after the rise of civilization, their role in some areas of the world became in part, at least, a negative one leading to destruction of the resources on which they depended.

The early civilizations that could regard people as so many units in a production process, which could turn humans into slaves to be bartered and sold, inevitably had scant regard for the peasants who worked the land, or the land that was worked, so long as they produced their tax or tribute. It was inevitable also that they would begin the long conflict with those who remained free—who still dwelled in the wilderness as hunters, or who went back and forth from the wild lands as nomadic pastoralists. Since the early history of Civilization was also marked by another new phenomenon in human development—organized warfare—it was capable of instructing those whom it oppressed. If the nomads learned warfare from the city folk, they learned it well. For thousands of years they were to sweep, periodically, from the wild lands and overthrow the empires of the "civilized." But Civilization was to have its revenge. The nomads who settled in the conquered lands themselves became "civilized."

From time to time in the history of early Civilization, land failure occurred. Too many livestock grazed on the watersheds from which the rivers of Mesopotamia drained, or perhaps farmers, moving to escape the pressures of life in the irrigated valleys, unwisely cultivated the dry hillslopes and allowed the soil to wash away. We know that forests were cut without care for the future. The cedars of Lebanon were carried away for the navies of Phoenicia and Egypt, for the temples of Solomon, and for the buildings of Babylon. No doubt goats followed the loggers to graze on the newly cut over lands and prevent forest regrowth. Precisely what caused the change cannot now be known, but the record of the change can still be read on the land. Once the forested mountains became denuded and bare, with little grass or soil, the rivers grew full of silt and the irrigation canals of Babylon, Chaldea, and Nineveh became choked and useless. Deserts grew where once was fertile farm or pastureland. Throughout the early homelands of civilization, land damage grew devastating and continued to spread.

"The lion and the lizard keep
the courts where Jamshyd gloried
and drank deep."

Today it has taken all of the technology and skill that modern civilization can muster to restore a part of the land that was fertile and productive in earlier times. Some perhaps can never be restored. Also if we seek the area where mankind and nature alike are in the most serious trouble, where millions of people in 1974 face starvation, where millions of livestock have already died, it is the same semiarid lands of the old homeland of Civilization. Stretching from beyond the Indus River in Pakistan, where the early civilization of Mohenjo Daro and Harappa once flourished, across through the Mesopotamian lands where civilization began, on through Egypt and across North Africa around the edges of the Sahara to where Mauritania and Morocco meet the Atlantic Ocean, man's uses of the land and its waters are out of balance with the capacity of the ecosystems to sustain them.

Nomadic Pastoralism

The semiarid grazing lands of Northern Africa and the Middle East are characterized by a cool, rainy winter followed by a long, dry period in late spring, summer, and autumn. Grasses and other herbaceous plants put out some initial growth after the first rains, but do most of their growing when the weather warms up in spring and the soil is still moist. They then bloom, set seed, and become dormant until late autumn or early winter brings more rain. Perennial grasses depend, for their early growth, on energy reserves stored in the roots and root crown. Once enough green leafage is produced, however, photosynthesis begins to exceed respiration and the plant can continue to grow on current energy production. Late in the growing season, however, it must have enough remaining leafage to store extra energy in the roots in order to permit growth to resume when the rains again fall. The nutritional value of the plant, as forage for livestock, reaches its peak early in the growing season and declines after seeds are set. During the summer when the leafage is cured and dry, some species maintain a reasonably high nutritional value, but others, usually less palatable to livestock, quickly decline to protein levels inadequate to sustain grazing animals.

If grazing is too heavy during the period of early growth, the plant must continue to draw on stored energy reserves to put out additional growth. If grazing continues these reserves can be exhausted, and the plant dies. If grazing is too heavy, late in the growing season and before the plant dries out, the plant will be unable to store sufficient energy to permit growth to get off to a good start in the next season. If it is too heavy before seeds are formed, reproduction may be prevented (except by vegetative means), even though the parent plant may survive.

Balancing livestock pressure with the carrying capacity of a dry rangeland is a skill that must be learned. Even a small number of animals grazing continuously in a small area can destroy the vegetation. Thus it is common to see bare areas around waterholes or wells where animals drink. Trampling by too many hooves in such areas can be as disastrous as, or more so than, grazing. Too early grazing usually creates a problem if animals are at all concentrated, since trampling of the wet soil compacts it and makes it less able to absorb moisture from future rains, and at this time the plants are least able to withstand grazing pressure. One way of achieving a balance on dry rangelands is to keep animals moving. Wild grazing animals move from place to place without being urged, and seldom put too much pressure on any one area of land—except where their numbers have become temporarily excessive. Some domestic breeds also move out and disperse, others however need be herded. Most animals, however, if not pressured will graze selectively—taking the most nutritious plants, or plant parts first, and will keep moving.

Originally, the nomadic way of life seemed well adapted to the grazing lands of the Mediterranean and Middle East. Animals and people kept moving. The high mountains were grazed during the late spring and summer, after growth was well advanced—since the growing season would start later with each increase in altitude—livestock could be kept on more nutritious forage for the longest period of time. Periods when livestock and people were relatively sedentary would usually coincide with the periods when the vegetation was dry and dormant and least likely to suffer damage. Along the desert edges, away from mountains, nomads tended to follow the rains, which in such areas are often localized rather than general. In all cases, animals were kept moving and not allowed to permanently damage any area. Heavily grazed spots were allowed to recover.

Livestock numbers were, to some degree, held in check by natural causes. Wild predators were about, and diseases and accidents took their toll. If drought did occur, nomads could move to higher rainfall areas or to wet areas along rivers or lake margins—but malnutrition would help to reduce herds that had exceeded grazing capacities.

With some peoples, excess animals were slaughtered for the tribal food supply, and others were sold or bartered for the products of agricultural lands. Other nomadic herdsmen, the Masai of Kenya, for example, did not either market or butcher their animals but used them only for milk, or by tapping their veins, for blood. For all nomads, however, domestic animals were not things to be primarily raised for commercial purposes, to be sold for cash, but were rather creatures tied in with the entire structure of society. They provided a way of life and had ceremonial, religious, and prestige value that far exceeded any economic concern. This was to create a problem, when European technology arrived on the scene with veterinary medicine and ideas about livestock sanitation, as well as the means for destroying predators and putting a halt to intertribal raiding. Livestock numbers naturally began to increase. This made the nomads happy at first. Unfortunately their lands did not increase, and because of increased grazing their carrying capacity declined. To add to the problem the division of the lands of the nomads, first among European colonies, and then among new nation states, further restricted the movements of those who had previously recognized no national boundaries. Nomadism became a "problem."

Some factors, however, operated to prevent disaster. The uneven distribution of potential watering places in these dry lands was one. Areas away from permanent water could only be grazed during the wet season when there was sufficient water in temporary ponds or seasonal streams. Thus their vegetation provided an emergency reserve—it could not be so readily overgrazed. Governments and international aid agencies, seeking to solve the nomadism problem, started to work to remove that final safeguard by a program of borehole drilling to bring up permanent water in these previously preserved areas. Freed from constraints, increased numbers of livestock could soon reduce the wet-season ranges to the same barren state as the overused lands near the old watering places (Dasmann et al., 1973).

Western-oriented, range-management specialists have torn out their hair over the nomadic grazing situation, since the concept of limiting livestock numbers to carrying capacities of rangelands seemed to escape the nomads. Traditionally they had never had to worry. Now they tended to feel that the problem was one forced on them by governments. Particularly they resented the spread of agricultural peoples into what had been their dry season reserves, the better watered lands along rivers and lakes, or for the Sahara-Sahel nomads, the higher rainfall savanna areas to the south.

Speaking of the Tuareg nomads, who center their movements in the Adrar n Iforas mountains in northern Mali, Jeremy Swift (1972, 1973) has pointed out why the conventional strategy of limiting herds to the carrying capacity of the environment does not work:

1.   Pasture and water are too scattered and vary too much from year to year to permit private ownership. The lands are owned communally, and shared with other tribes. If the Tuareg reduce their herds, others may increase theirs and the Tuareg will suffer. There is no incentive for herd reduction.

2.   The Tuareg have few cash needs and there is no incentive to sell more animals than the minimum needed for tea, tobacco, cloth, sugar, and grain.

3.   Animals are kept mostly for milk, transport, and social rating, although some young animals may be slaughtered or bartered.

4.   Social prestige and social security is provided by loaning animals out to other members of the extended tribe. Since different families graze their animals in different locations this reduces the likelihood that all will be affected by any one disaster. The more animals out on loan, the better able one family will be to regain their status if their herds should die off.

5.   Limiting herds to a carrying capacity that fluctuates widely from year to year would demand a market mechanism for disposing of excess stock in bad years and buying additional stock for good years. This does not exist. Markets are too remote.

6.   In the past there were fewer people, more land, and movements were not restricted. This has changed. Algeria and Niger are no longer freely accessible to nomads from Mali. However, traditional cultures cannot change so quickly.

The result has been a growing ecological disaster that is now being brought to its final stages by the continued Sahelian drought. To add to this, the wildlife of the region, which once provided an emergency reserve for the Tuareg during drought seasons, has been depleted by steady poaching and general slaughter by military forces, oil prospectors, and other outsiders.

It is difficult to see a future for the nomads of the Sahel. Too many have already died. Their herds have largely vanished. The vegetation that supported them has been destroyed over large areas. The Sahara desert moves outward into the old grazing lands. Perhaps, if and when the rains come, the survivors—greatly reduced in numbers and with fewer animals—will have a chance to come back. Perhaps.

Grazing in Other Lands

The problem of managing grazing animals on grasslands, savannas, scrublands, or other dry areas is not confined to southwest Asia and north Africa, but extends to Asia. Africa, Australia, North and South America, and Mediterranean Europe. Unfortunately, in the past, most of the experts in animal husbandry and pasture management who were to give advice to the peoples of Asia or Africa had received their training in northern and western Europe where dry rangelands do not exist and the problems are quite different. The close cropping that works well on well-watered lawns or their pasture equivalents creates havoc in steppe and dry savanna.

It is argued by some food scientists today that the best way to handle the problem of domestic animals is to eliminate the animals—since feeding them wastes protein and energy that could otherwise be obtained directly by man through a vegetable diet. In other words, the operation of food chains, with their pyramids of biomass and energy, and the necessary loss between trophic levels, means that far fewer human carnivores can be supported than human herbivores. If the object is to support the greatest number of people, and we are feeding corn to hogs, instead of eating the corn ourselves, then the argument has merit. Georg Borgstrom (1973), for example, has pointed out that we confuse the picture in comparing the calories contained in the diet of a vegetarian Indian with the diet of a meat-eating American. To show the contrast properly we would need to add to the calories directly consumed by the American the calories consumed by the domestic animals that provided him with meat. This would show an enormous imbalance in caloric food consumption between the rich and the poor nations of the world.

However, we are not concerned here with the question of feeding corn to hogs, regardless of the merits one way or the other, but with the use of the dry rangelands of the world. Without irrigation, these lands can be used for the production of farm crops only at great risk of totally destroying them. If their natural vegetation is removed, and if they are plowed and cultivated, crops may be produced in those years when rainfall is high. But these years will inevitably be followed by a longer string of years when rainfall is well below average. In these dry years crops will fail, and the soil will be left exposed to blowing by wind. We have had many examples of land-use failure resulting from this practice. It is a likely contributor to the decline of some of the ancient empires and human populations of the middle East. It was a major contributor to land destruction in the American Middle West during the Dust Bowl years of the 1930s and again in the 1950s. During wet years rangelands had been plowed in western Kansas, Nebraska, Oklahoma, Colorado, Texas, and the Dakotas. When dry years returned the farms were destroyed, the farmers ruined financially, and an expensive federally supported program of rangeland restoration was required.

It can be argued that farming need not fail on such lands, if the kind of care characteristic of the best quality peasant agriculture is provided. The Nabatean civilization of the Negev Desert in Israel was supported by agriculture carried out where the rainfall was usually less than 5 inches a year. But every possible means of water collection and conservation was employed and the lands were cared for continually by people who were not particularly oriented toward a cash or market economy, nor in driving to Jerusalem to take in the week-end's entertainment (Evanari, et al., 1971). Even so, the Nabateans fell victim, as would most farmers of other areas where ancient civilizations held sway, to the ebb and flow of migrating peoples, to wars and revolution. When the social structure is disrupted by the crises of nations, and people are forced from the land—the farms will not wait their return. Wind or water carries the soil away.

In the absence of the kind of intensive land care that is required, the dry lands of the world can be brought into food production by converting their forage into meat and other animal products. These animal products may be provided by wildlife or domestic animals. There are convincing arguments that it is more profitable economically, and ecologically sound to maintain these lands as wildlife areas (Dasmann, 1964). But the skills for managing wild animals disappeared with people that once practiced them, and are only today being slowly and laboriously relearned by wildlife scientists and managers. There are few of these. For most governments and most peoples it seems easier to go the domestic animal route since the skills for handling these animals have not yet been forgotten in the countries of the Third World, and are being advanced to a high level of sophistication in the economically wealthy countries.

(I cannot resist a side point here that contradicts, in part, the first sentence of the preceding paragraph. In the Great Basin and Southwestern Deserts of America, the Utes, Paiutes, Pimas, and other Indian peoples could and did harvest the wild plants and convert them directly into eatable food, just as the Kalahari Bushmen, the Australian aborigines, and other desert-dwelling hunter-gatherers have done elsewhere. But for the technological world these skills have been forgotten, and are only kept alive to the extent that they have not been entirely lost in various submerged groups.)

The management of domestic animals on dry rangelands, despite the scientific and managerial skills that are potentially available, continues to cause trouble in even the most scientifically oriented cultures. Scientists usually do not own or lease the rangelands, and those who do are forced to be part of a market economy, unless their ranch is kept to provide a hobby or a source of tax deductions from income earned elsewhere. As part of a market economy, those who raise livestock on the dry lands of America can be divided into two extreme groups: those who want to make as much profit as quickly as possible, and then sell out; and those who genuinely enjoy the management of land and livestock and would like to maintain or enhance the productivity of both. The former tend to close at least one ear when listening to good advice on how to keep their rangelands in good order. The latter are a joy to work with, and have carried out remarkable feats of rangeland restoration in many parts of America.

America's rangelands went through a period of destructive exploitation, characterized by a "population explosion" among domestic livestock during pioneer days. Private rangelands were reasonably well cared for, but most of America's western range was public domain—government land, commonly owned and exploited. The damage done to that land during the 70 years from 1860 to 1930 has in many areas yet to be repaired. A report by the Forest Service (1936) pointed out that the average carrying capacity of the western range of the United States had been reduced 50 percent. For the public domain, the percentage reduction was greater. Some areas had lost all of their soil and were down to bedrock. Others were carved and washed away by deep gullies. Erosion was everywhere, and deserts had spread. Despite opposition from livestock owners, the National Forest rangelands have been greatly improved from that low ebb, and some of the Public Domain, now managed by the Federal Bureau of Land Management has been brought back. However, efforts by the more exploitative variety of livestock owner to obtain complete control over the government rangelands continue. Most do not want to take over private ownership of these lands, with the tax obligations and other problems that this involves. They essentially want the right to do as they please without interference from the custodians.

The Use of Tropical Forest Regions

If the warm, dry lands of the world represent one of the major areas of conservation concern, their opposite in terms of humidity, the hot wet lands represent the other. Throughout the humid tropical forests of the world the destructive impact of technocratic pressure is being felt most strongly, so that there is serious concern that the tropical rain forests may cease to exist as one of the world's biotic regions, except for those few patches saved in parks and reserves, or too inaccessible to be used in any way. Yet these are the regions of the greatest biotic complexity and diversity in which most of the species of the world's land animals and plants find their home. The loss of the rain forests would be an irreparable disaster since there is increasing evidence that in their primary form they represent a nonrenewable resource (Gomez Pompa et al., 1972).

Tropical rain forests originally had their greatest extent in Latin America, from southern Mexico through Central America and down the Colombian coast, to join with the main mass of forest stretching for thousands of miles through the basins of the Amazon and Orinoco Rivers. In Africa they were also extensive, all through the basin of the Zaire River and up the Guinea coast. From India and Ceylon eastward through Southeast Asia and out along the islands to New Guinea and the Philippines was the third major area of their development. Australia has a narrow patch of tropical forest, and various derivatives of humid tropical forest occur in the smaller tropical islands of the world. In all of these places they have been much battered, and are now under serious threat.

Man was not a forest species, and only a few groups of people have thoroughly adapted to life in the tropical forests—the pygmies of the Ituri Forest in Congo are an example. For the most part, people have succeeded in living in tropical forests by clearing small areas in which food crops could be grown, while at the same time taking advantage of whatever wild produce and animal life could be obtained. Because of the nature of the soils and vegetation in most tropical forest areas, such clearings were only temporary and were usually abandoned after a few years of planting, to be replaced by fresh clearings. This original pattern of shifting agriculture, known as *milpa* in Mexico, *ladang* in Malaysia, *chitemene* in Zambia has supported forest peoples over thousands of years. It was a successful adaptation to forest ecosystems for so long as the number of people remained small and the area of forest available for clearing remained large.

Tropical forests appear burgeoning and luxuriant and on the surface give the impressions of support from rich and fertile soils. In most areas, however, these impressions are misleading. Most mineral nutrients are tied up in the vegetation and in a layer of surface litter and humus. Cycling of nutrients is rapid, as are all biological processes in warm, humid environments. Dead plants or animals decompose quickly and the chemicals in their bodies are quickly picked up to flow through new food chains. There is little surplus to filter through and enrich the soils. Beneath the vegetation and litter many of the soil types in tropical forests are relatively devoid of plant nutrients. Usually they are rich only in the iron and aluminum salts that give them a reddish color, and earn the name of ferralsol for one of the more widespread soil types. By cutting these forests, burning the debris, and then cultivating the soil, one can produce crops for a short period of time—during the time when the nutrients previously held in the wild vegetation are still available. With heavy rainfall, however, these soon leach out of the reach of crop roots. In cleared areas organic materials on the soil quickly break down, and their nutrients in turn must be used or wash away. Thus shifting agriculture makes sense, if the cleared spots are small. Once abandoned these are quickly invaded by the trees and shrubs best able to grow on such open, mineral deficient areas. These in turn allow for reinvasion by the less tolerant species of the mature forest. The forest in time repairs the damage done by clearing, and the surface mineral cycling is restored (Janzen, 1973).

Shifting agriculture, however, must have a long-term rotation period that allows adequate time for forest restoration. If it is crowded by too much people pressure, or by the destruction of forest through the encroachment of civilization, then plots must be returned to and cleared once more before recovery has taken place. Fertility rapidly declines, crop yields go down, soils wash away or are baked into hard laterite, and the people must give up and move out.

There are areas in the tropical forest region where different conditions occur. These are where the soils have been built up and are periodically restored through volcanic action—the drifting and settling of volcanic ash—and can be cultivated without danger of quick depletion of fertility. The civilizations of southeast Asia have been built from such volcanic soils, along with some other soils that are more inherently fertile. Permanent agriculture has been sustained over thousands of years and has been highly productive in these regions. It has involved, however, intensive care. Soils are continually restored and kept in good tilth by the addition of organic wastes. Mixed plantings of perennials serve to keep the soil screened from the destructive influence of direct sun and rain. Irrigation, usually combined with terracing, helps to counteract the high transpiration rates that occur in hot climates, as well as to prevent erosion.

Great agricultural success has been achieved with paddy rice in the alluvial soils that develop in the river basins that drain out of rich, volcanic areas. In southeast Asia, rice fields have remained in production for four thousand years or more. However, similar success cannot be expected where the alluvium is built up from soils that wash from more sterile uplands—ferralsols up hill do not change into rich valley soils when they are carried into river basins.

Considerable success also has been achieved in areas with moderately fertile soils through the use of tree plantations, or shrubs such as coffee, with trees left for an overstory. Such plantations more closely resemble the original forest and provide some of its functions by way of shading and adding litter to the surface soil. However, the more fertile tropical forest lands were, with some exceptions, settled long ago. The remaining tropical forest, which we are concerned today, occurs on soils that cannot be readily turned into productive croplands—or only with an enormous input of hand care and attention to their protection and restoration (Dasmann et al., 1973).

Today the onslaught against the tropical forests is based on a variety of reasons. In South America it is part of a drive to open up the country and tie it into one economic unit through construction of major highways into the interior. As the roads proceed and land becomes accessible, logging and clearing of forests take place. The cleared land is frequently taken over, temporarily by peasants, particularly those driven from already overcrowded areas of depleted soils. Much of it is purchased by wealthy individuals to be used as cattle ranches. For this purpose it is cleared, burned, and seeded to grass. For a time, until the soil fertility is depleted, or scrub invasion gets out of hand, it can produce cattle. This is usually sufficient for the original purchaser to sell out for a good profit. After a short while, however, the productivity will inevitably experience a rapid decline. It may then be sold to landless farmers who will attempt to wring a bare living from it until its fertility is completely exhausted. Where such clearing is widespread, there is little opportunity for the original forest to become restored, and at best it would require centuries for this to happen. Degraded scrub replaces the original forest luxuriance (Smith, 1971).

In Southeast Asia, and in particular in Indonesia, foreign lumber companies are the principal exploiters. Governments sell out timber rights, in order to gain quick income, usually with little or no restriction on the activities of the timber operators and no requirement for reforestation or care of the land. The loggers in turn take everything that can be profitably turned into pulp, chips, lumber, or any other forest product, and leave a scene of devastation behind. Once again the poor peasant follows to attempt to scratch a living from what is left. Where the soils happen to be fertile and able to sustain agriculture, the conversion to farm land from forest may be worthwhile. Too often, however, the forests that remain cover soils of low fertility and the agricultural endeavor is likely to fail.

The problem of managing diverse tropical forests, where hundreds of different tree species may occur on a few acres, to obtain a sustained yield of forest products without damage to the environment is a difficult one. In most areas only low intensity use seems compatible with forest stability, and this has little appeal to those who wish to get high returns from a high investment in road building, timber cutting, log hauling, and processing machinery. However, the greatest value of the forests over the long run lies in their biological diversity. They are reservoirs of genetic materials, the scientific and ecological value of which has been but slightly investigated. Perhaps most of all they are reservoirs of wilderness and guarantors of biosphere stability. But these qualities do not yield a cash return.

One can no longer hope for very much, since the rate of attack on the forests is accelerating. One can hope, however, that sufficient areas will be left alone to protect the native peoples who have traditionally depended on them, and to provide a refuge for the diversity of wild animal and plant life of the forest region. One must ask that the long term security of life on earth not be sacrificed for today's profits. But the big machines are moving and time is short.

Other Areas

Although no form of land is safe against destructive exploitation, some areas are more vulnerable than others. Among these, four categories are under serious attack at the present time: islands, high mountains, coastal estuaries, and the tundras of the Arctic. Islands and high mountains share similar qualities. Both provide refuges for unique species and both are unusually vulnerable to outside disturbance. Because of isolation over long periods of time, islands and high mountains tend to become separate centers of evolution, and consequently become the homes of endemic species—those that occur in no other area. Because of their isolation, however, such species usually lack the ability to maintain themselves in competition with alien species brought in by man's activities. Therefore, if one examines the lists of threatened species of plant and animal life, the greatest degree of endangerment, as well as the highest rates of extinction, will be found in the more isolated islands. High mountains, although until recently not subject to great human interference, will probably soon take second place in the number of species threatened with extinction. Along with the wild biota, human populations endemic to islands, with cultures developed in isolation from others, are also highly vulnerable to outside interference with the result that now most have been modified beyond recognition, even where the people themselves have managed to survive. Mountain peoples have been affected less, thus far, but are equally vulnerable. Both islands and mountains, although subject to various pressures in the past, are now particularly endangered by massive waves of tourism, made up of people who are seeking the unique, the exotic, or looking for suitable environments for skiing, surfing, skindiving and other outdoor activities. As the continental areas become more overcrowded and battered, the remote islands and mountains gain greater appeal.

The estuaries and coastal regions of the world, the places where fresh water meets salt, and land meets sea, have always been the nursery grounds, sheltering places, and sources of nutrients for the marine life of the oceans. They also have become the most popular areas for development—for industries that benefit from water transportation or require large amounts of water for cooling, for shipping and transportation as well as recreational boating, for home sites and recreation sites, or simply as dumping grounds for pollutants. As such they are among the world's most endangered habitats, and consequently there is a growing threat to the long-term productivity of the oceans. One cannot ask that all development along estuaries and coastal waters be brought to a halt. It is necessary, however, to demand that development in such areas be brought under the most careful planning and control, so that the long-range values of lands and waters at the edge of the sea be adequately protected.

The Arctic tundras until recently were regarded as one of the last areas on earth likely to be subjected to massive development activities. Now their remoteness and isolation has vanished, their animal and plant life has been brought under threat, and their long-term stability must be seriously considered. Although the greatest publicity accompanied the discovery of oil on the Arctic slope of Alaska, and the long legal controversy that attended the decision to build an oil pipeline across the tundra, over the Brooks Range, and down to the port of Valdez, similar threats occur in Canada—notably the James Bay project—and in the Arctic lands of the Soviet Union—including the decision to reverse the flow of major rivers draining into the Arctic Ocean. The native peoples of these lands have long suffered from the impact of civilization, and only recently have their land rights received any degree of consideration. For the most part their cultures have been warped out of shape, so that the old ways are forgotten while they remain out of place in a technocratic society.

General Considerations

For all these lands, and for all lands on earth there are some general principles by which we may guide the plans for future use. First, where preindustrial land-use systems exist, with a long history of successful adaptation to their environments and continuing productivity, they should, if possible, be left alone. This applies to hunter-gatherers, nomadic pastoralists, and traditional agriculturalists, as well as other variants of these cultures. Where, however, interference has already taken place, or must inevitably occur—then attention must be paid to the total land-use system in combination with the social system, the means for population control, and all other facets of the economy. It is dangerous and destructive to interfere with part of the system—for example, to provide veterinary care for livestock, or water developments in previously waterless areas—without equal attention to the other parts of the system—for example, agreements and means for limiting livestock numbers, or for controlling grazing pressure. If a successful system must be changed then it must be replaced with something better that has the same checks and balances, the same ecological basis, and is likely to be socially acceptable.

Successful use and management of dry grazing lands have resulted from both the traditional practices of nomadic pastoralism, and from modern, scientifically based ranching in North America, Australia, and other areas dominated by urban-industrial civilization. A hybrid of the two systems, however, is likely to fail.

Highly successful land-use practices are most likely to be found in areas where the people who manage the land live on the land and are responsive to its needs. It is the indigenous people, those who belong to the land, who are best qualified to manage it and control its use. It is the invader, the outsider, the alien who causes trouble. This is partly because he is not familiar with the ecosystems he is attempting to change, he is not responsive to that particular land and its life. More than that, however, it is because the invader is a transient. He does not believe that he will have to depend, or his children, depend on the land he is using. Instead he is intent on draining its resources to build security in some other area—in the city, or in another country.

At this time, there is no way we can force exploiters to live their lives on the lands they exploit. We do, however, need some equally effective ways of controlling their behavior. General principles of control need to take into consideration the question of whether or not the proposed or existing use can be sustained. If it cannot be sustained use then it becomes destructive use, and it must be either prohibited or modified. All proposed changes in existing forms of land use, where the existing forms are successful, or show evidence of continuing success, must be subjected to careful ecological and sociological evaluation. Unless the change can show benefits that far outweigh any potential damages, it should normally be rejected—since the risks involved in such changes cannot be totally evaluated. In other words, negative effects are likely to be underestimated, whereas positive economic benefits are commonly overestimated.

The question of who is to exercise control over land use also needs careful consideration. In general, it would be expected that those who live in the area, the local community, are in the best condition to judge whether or not a particular form of land use has long-term acceptability. However, this would apply only to land-use changes that have only local, and not regional or national consequences. We need move higher up the ladder of responsibility, to the regional, the state, or the national level as the costs or benefits of the particular form of land use have wider significance. In doing so, however, the interests of those likely to be negatively effected by the continuance of a particular land-use practice, or the introduction of a new form of land use, will require consideration. Where the decision is made to go ahead, regardless of these negative effects, then those affected must be adequately compensated.

One cannot see a very bright future, however, regardless of institutional controls, unless there is a change in attitude toward land. So long as it is regarded as a mere commodity whose value is to be judged only in the market place, we will continue to destroy the earth on which we depend. When land is regarded as the home for people and other living things, as the sole base for humanity's future—then there will be hope.

References

Borgstrom, Georg, 1973. Food, feed, and energy. *Ambio*, 2:214–219.

Dasmann, R. F., 1964. *African game ranching*. Pergamon, Oxford.

Dasmann, R. F., J. P. Milton, and P. Freeman, 1973. *Ecological principles for economic development*. Wiley, Ltd., London.

Evanari, M., L. Shanan, and N. Tadmor, 1971. *The Negev—The challenge of a desert*. Harvard University Press, Cambridge.

Farvar, M. Taghi, and J. P. Milton, 1972. *The careless technology*. Natural History Press, New York.

Forest Service, 1936. *The western range*. Senate Document 199, Washington, D.C.

Gomez Pompa, A., C. Vazquez-Yanes, S. Guevara, 1972. The tropical rainforest: a non-renewable resource. *Science, 177*:762–765.

Janzen, Daniel H., 1973. Tropical agroecosystems. *Science, 182*:1212–1219.

Lee, R. B., and I. DeVore, 1968. *Man the hunter*. Aldine, Chicago.

Neel, James V., 1970. Lessons from a "primitive" people. *Science, 170*:815–822.

Sauer, Carl O., 1950. Grassland climax, fire, and man. *Journal of Range Management, 3*:16–21.

Smith, Antony, 1971. *Mato Grosso*. Dutton, New York.

Swift, Jeremy, 1972. *Pastoral nomadism as a form of land use: the Tuareg of the Adrar n Iforas (Mali)*. Proc. Intern. African Inst. Seminar on pastoral nomadism in Africa. Sussex University, Mimeo.

Swift, Jeremy, 1973. Disaster and a Sahelian nomad economy. *Drought in Africa*. Centre for African Studies, University of London, pp. 71–78.

Waller, Robert, 1971. Out of the Garden of Eden. *New Scientist, 54*:528–530.

chapter seven

The Dwindling of Diversity

"Let these be encouraged: Gnostics, hip Marxists, Teilhard de Chardin Catholics, Druids, Taoists, Biologists, Witches, Yogins, Bhikkus, Quakers, Sufis, Tibetans, Zens, Shamans, Bushmen, American Indians, Polynesians, Anarchists, Alchemists . . . the list is long. All primitive cultures, all communal and ashram movements."

Gary Snyder and Friends, *Four changes*

Ethnocide

October 12, 1492 may well become the "day that will live in infamy" should any humane history of the world be written. On that day millions of people belonging to thousands of cultures who inhabited two of the world's continents and their surrounding islands were exposed for the first time to a fanatically religious, somewhat mad, rapacious group of invaders from a half-civilized peninsula of Eurasia. Tragically enough, the people, to be remembered as Arawaks, of the island to be called San Salvador, welcomed Columbus and his crew. Soon they and their kindred on all the islands of the Caribbean were dead (Sauer, 1964).

There were other infamous days, such as in 1519 when Hernando Cortés and his fellow brigands were greeted by the people who lived at a place to

129

be called Vera Cruz in a country to be known as Mexico. Soon afterwards one of the world's strangest and most remarkable civilizations was destroyed, most of its people killed, and most of its records and artifacts pillaged or burned. Perhaps worse was the arrival of the treacherous Francisco Pizarro in the land of the Inca in 1530, since the Andean mountain civilization that he destroyed was truly unique, and the people he butchered were unusually talented.

Elsewhere in the world the sequence of tragic days was to be repeated. Captain James Cook was, on the whole, a good man, but his arrival in Tahiti on 13 April, 1769 marked the beginning of the end for peoples and cultures throughout the Pacific. On April 22, 1770 the unfortunate aborigines of Australia first sighted Cook's sails, and with them, for most of their people, the doom of everything that they had been or might have become (Burdick, 1961; Melville, 1961; Moorehead, 1966).

After World War II when it was found that Adolf Hitler and his followers had put to death six million Jews in Europe, the word genocide—the murder of whole genetically similar groups of people—came into the popular vocabulary. Since then the word ethnocide, the destruction of cultures, has been added to describe another aspect of the problem. It is nothing new. Perhaps since the Stone Age there has been a tendency for one group of people to crowd out, change, or destroy another group with different ways or a different appearance. In historical times a sort of grisly fame was achieved by the Mongols under Genghis Khan and the Tartars under Tamerlane for their destruction of empires and of peoples who opposed them. Yet these conquering horsemen from Asia were not particularly intolerant of different cultures or different races, providing only that these people would submit to their overlordship and pay tribute.

It remained for the followers of two religions of western Asia, the Moslems who followed Muhammad and the Christians who followed Christ to set new standards of ferocity in their opposition to all who did not bow down and promise to be faithful to the Crescent or the Cross. Indeed the belief was expressed that those who were not of the "true religion" were better off dead. Although the religious impetus to convert or slay was modified with time, the belief that it is more permissible to maim, kill, or torture people who differ from you markedly in appearance or culture than to behave this way toward people of your own kind has persisted as recently as the Vietnam war.

Ethnic diversity developed over the hundreds of thousands of years of human cultural evolution because people lived in geographically isolated groups in areas with different environments. With increases in human numbers, with improved transportation, and with means of communication this isolation inevitably broke down. It also was inevitable that cultural differences would also break down as one group learned from another techniques, art forms, or ways of living that appeared more successful or were more easily practiced. Yet the culture that appears superior under one set of environmental or economic circumstances will not necessarily continue to be superior when circumstances change. Many civilizations have fallen into dust, whereas people who must have seemed backward and inferior to the city dwellers persisted in their "primitive" ways and in time gave rise to new and technologically superior cultures. The protection of cultural variety on earth is one way of insuring that the human race will continue to survive, as well as a way of providing for a more interesting and colorful existence. It further offers freedom for those who may not care to follow, for example, the ways of life available in an advanced technological society (Neel, 1970; Wilkinson, 1973).

There is little doubt, however, that antagonism, scorn, or indifference characterizes the attitudes of many people toward those who differ from them. It was almost inconceivable to a nineteenth century European or American that anyone could prefer ways of living different from his own, and the "blessings" of industrial civilization were forced on other cultures with the same fervor that Christianity was dispersed a few centuries earlier. It is inconceivable to many of today's technocrats that "primitive" peoples might have some insights regarding man's role in the universe that the technological world has lost, or that it could be better for humanity if these people were left alone. But, unfortunately, few people remain outside the web of modern technology.

The destruction of most of the people and cultures of the Americas by the European invaders is one of the saddest chapters in world history. Admittedly much of it took place as a sort of random "side effect" of the movement of Europeans into regions inhabited by people who had lived for thousands of years in isolation from the rest of the world. The Indians had little or no resistance to the diseases of Europe, and those that were harmless or nearly so to Europeans—the common cold or measles—became killing plagues among those who had no immunity. The Spanish in the West Indies would have preferred that the Indians remained alive, since they desired slaves, but they were unsuccessful in keeping them that way. Introduced diseases were no doubt aggravated in their effects by the cultural disruption and the psychological shock caused by the invaders. The tribes that were most friendly and peaceful were usually the hardest hit. Those that were hostile and warlike from the start often hung on a little longer, such as the Caribs who still are represented by a few survivors on the island of Dominica (Sauer, 1964).

However, much of the killing and disruption was deliberate. Diseases such as smallpox were deliberately spread. Entire tribes were massacred, with little or no excuse except the belief stated by General Sheridan, of Civil War fame, that "The only good Indians I ever saw were dead." There seems little doubt today that much of the killing of whites by Indians, although this was often gruesome enough, took place only after the tribe involved had been provoked beyond endurance. Treaties that had been signed in the most solemn manner between the Indian nations and the government of the United States were commonly broken, or set aside, while the Indians were still studying their terms and conditions (Brown, 1970).

Throughout the Americas some of the Indians survived, but usually in reduced numbers, and often with their cultural integrity shattered and much of their old folk knowledge lost. They were not without their spokesmen. Black Elk, of the Sioux, has told it well (Neihardt, 1932):

> "I did not know then how much was ended. When I look back now from this high hill of my old age, I can still see the butchered women and children lying heaped and scattered all along the crooked gulch, as plain as when I saw them with eyes still young. And I can see that something else died there in the bloody mud, and was buried in the blizzard. A people's dream died there. It was a beautiful dream . . . the nation's hoop is broken and scattered. There is no center any longer, and the sacred tree is dead."

So he recalled the last massacre of his people at a place called Wounded Knee in December, 1891.

There is no point in weeping over events of the distant past, nor any value in condemning people of past generations for acts whose significance was scarcely understood in the cultural context of the time. The important thing is that the process still continues. Today, as in the past, the destruction of cultures and ways of life goes on, and in some places it is still accompanied by the murder of the peoples involved. It is not that the destruction necessarily represents a firm policy on the part of governments, although in some places it may. More often, however, it represents the lack of a policy, a failure to confront and consider the issue at all, a belief that the problem will take care of itself, will go away. Unfortunately, the problem does go away. The people die, or their ways are forgotten. Failure to take a position or to determine a policy then becomes a policy in itself, a policy against those people and cultures not yet assimilated into, or resistant against, the technological world.

The Brazilian Example

The process that goes on can be examined through the recent experience of Brazil. Brazil is unusual in that until recently most of its land was remote, largely untouched wilderness. Its principal population, larger than that of any other Latin American country, had been confined to a relative small proportion of the land. The dense rain forests of the Amazon were essentially undisturbed. Inhabiting this wilderness were Indian tribes who had, in some instances, not encountered any Europeans or representatives of the ruling or officially recognized societies of Brazil. Others had encountered people from the outside, but had chased them away, fought them off, or retreated from further contact. Essentially they remained members of their own free nations who owed no allegiance to Brazil, and indeed had never heard of Brazil (Bates, 1910; Neel, 1970; A. Smith, 1971).

The world of today, however, operates on the basis of popularly accepted myths and one of these is the sovereignty of nation-states. According to this, a certain area of the globe is recognized, by other nation-states, as being the property of a particular nation-state. Within that area the authority of the state is not to be questioned. Since each nation-state is required to have a national government, if for no other purpose than to deal with other nation states, such governments are formed whether or not they are needed or appropriate. They may consist of a hereditary monarch such as the Emperor of Ethiopia, a military dictator who has risen to power behind the guns and tanks of the army, such as Generalissimo Francisco Franco of Spain, or more rarely a democratically elected government. Even the latter, however, is seldom, if ever, representative of all of the people or groups in a country. Regardless of how representative or democratic, the government can exercise authority over the people of the state by force of army or police if not by less physically coercive means. Furthermore, in international law, because of the accepted fiction that the government in truth represents the nation, nobody may intervene in the internal affairs of the nation state no matter how morally outraged they may be by the treatment handed out to peoples or ethnic groups within the boundary of that particular state. In Ruanda or Burundi the Hutu or the Tutsi may decide to wipe each other out. Although tens of thousands of people are massacred by the group in power, the United Nations can only wring its collective hands, and nations can only write letters of protest, if they dare to do that much. Any people who happen to be trapped inside a line drawn on a map, perhaps by a pope in the fifthteenth century, and are therefore considered residents of what is to be known as an independent nation-state may be in for a rough time unless they can become the dominant group and seize power. In Brazil the Indians are not dominant and have no power.

It is not the official policy of Brazil that is particularly unenlightened. In the past Brazil has made various efforts to protect its Indians and has, for example, designated large areas of the country as integral reserves for the tribes that inhabited them. Areas such as the 2,200,000 hectare Rio Xingu reserve or the 2,500,000 hectare Tucumacque Reserve were in theory at least areas in which the Indians would be free from outside interference (IUCN, 1973). But interference is hard to prevent in a region as large, as difficult to patrol, and as sparsely inhabited as the interior of Brazil. In many respects Amazonas and the Mato Grosso have resembled the old Wild West of the United States. Indians were often slaughtered or otherwise damaged by people who were operating outside the law. Harm was also done by well-intentioned missionaries who carried the viruses and bacteria of physical disease as well as the more insidious virus of technological culture, which destroyed the health and vitality of the native culture. As also was true in the history of North America, the official agency charged with the welfare of Indians was often venal and corrupt, or at other times inept, and rarely effective or enlightened in protecting its clients (A. Smith, 1971; N. Smith, 1971; O'Shaughnessy, 1973).

In the 1970s the finish of the still remote peoples of Brazil is coming near. New highways are being pushed into the interior as part of a trans-Amazonian system that will connect all parts of the country to the capital and the coast. Following the road builders come the settlers, poor peasants from the arid northeast of the country, or cowboys and other employees of the wealthy who have bought large sections of rainforest for the purpose of destroying it and replacing it with cattle pastures. The Indians still fight back, or retreat to wilder areas, but the fights are always lost and soon there will be no wilderness to retreat to. Only a strictly enforced government policy to set aside, deed over to the tribes that live there, and strictly maintain Indian lands where these people can live without interference can bring any hope for their future (O'Shaughnessy, 1973).

Brazil is singled out not because it is the worst, but because it is the largest and most dramatic example of the damaging impact of technological culture on peoples with other ways of life. Furthermore, Brazil has attempted to protect its indigenous people. Many other countries have not.

A Program for "Peripheral Peoples"

It is today considered morally unacceptable that one dominant group of people should exterminate another group who differ racially, genetically, or culturally from the dominant group. The world community as represented by the United Nations does not condone such behavior. Nevertheless member states of the United Nations continue to practice genocide. Furthermore, it is considered as almost virtuous for members of the dominant urban-industrial culture of the world to extend the benefits of this culture to peoples who have previously lived outside of it. That this extension of technological culture leads to the disruption and often the total destruction of the culture of the people to be "benefitted" is considered at worst a regrettable but necessary circumstance. In the name of providing medical service, sanitation, more food, clothing, modern housing, or other material benefits of urban-industrial society it is considered permissible to destroy the spirit and reason for living of the people to be provided for.

It is sometimes pointed out that you "can't keep people in zoos" or make museum specimens of them even if the zoos or museums are large natural reserves. Admittedly it would be as bad not to allow people the freedom to change, to take their part in technological society, as it would be to force this change upon them. However, such a danger is far more often advanced in conversation than it is to be found in reality and appears to be a standard argument of those who wish to change others "for their own good." There are no examples of people who are overprotected, but countless examples of people who have been destroyed.

It is particularly ironic and disturbing that in the 1970s many of the people of the so-called Third World, who have only recently escaped from colonial domination, are ruthless or negligent in their treatment of minority ethnic groups and show little concern for the freedom or rights of those who do not hold the reins of power. The Iraqis make war on their Kurdish people, the dominant groups in Chad have pursued the nomads of their north with the aid of the French army, whereas in the Sudan the dominant groups have fought a long and bitter war against the southern non-Moslem peoples. That such an unfortunate outcome of the "national wars of liberation" was predicted by one of their theoretical architects, Frantz Fanon, and could therefore have been avoided makes this form of persecution even less excusable.

There is no easy way to protect people of what have been called the "peripheral" cultures of this world, but certain steps have been recommended. One is to give them full title to the lands that they have traditionally possessed, or legal rights to the use of lands that they have traditionally visited for hunting, grazing, or other purposes. A second is to declare a hands-off policy for those lands. This does not mean that the people would in any way be prevented from jointing the central culture, or from changing their own ways of living. It would mean, however, that within their own lands these people would have the right to exclude all visitors, including missionaries and anthropologists. There are many other steps to be taken, but their direction should be determined by the "peripheral peoples" themselves. They alone have the right to determine their own future (*Ecologist,* 1972).

Ways of Life

A determination of the United Nations, which represents for the most part the dominant technological society, to provide security and tenure to the members of those ethnic groups that now represent the "endangered species" of human societies would go a long way toward preserving cultural diversity and maintaining ways of life that can have long term value for humanity. But it would not go far enough. If the Sioux and Cheyenne were given back the lands that were stolen from them in violation of treaties it would be a notable and honorable deed. But it would not bring back the buffalo hunters to the plains. If the heritage of the Incas was restored to the Andean Indians it would not breathe life back into Macchu Pichu. Cultures that have died are not easily reincarnated. But it is not too late to protect ways of life that have proved vital and enduring throughout all of human history, and these ways of life are also endangered even where they are practiced by members of the dominant ethnic group in a nation. The influence of technological society has become all-embracing and it does not spare those whose life styles do not fit the criteria of economic efficiency.

As we steer our way through the perilous decades that mark the closing of the twentieth century there is no reason to feel secure concerning the future of technological society. It has proven remarkably adaptable in the past, and for its elite groups has provided a degree of economic well-being undreamed of in early centuries, but its record of stewardship over the resources of the biosphere has been dismal indeed. Since the future of mankind depends on the continued availability of such resources, it would appear at least prudent to make provision for ways of life that are less dependent on destructive use of increasingly scarce resources. There are still present on earth hunting folk and fishing folk, nomadic herdsmen, subsistence farmers, and a variety of workers in the arts and crafts who require no great input, if any, of scarce fuels or industrial raw materials to perpetuate their ways of life. The skills that these people possess are a valuable part of the human heritage, their ways of life provide an alternative to technocracy. The skills, however, are being lost and the space in which they could be practiced is being crowded (Neel, 1970; Swift, 1972; Waller, 1971).

There has always been a tendency among some people to reject the ways of technocracy and to seek simpler and more satisfying life styles. During the eighteenth century, when industrialized society was in its youth, the Romantic poets, artists, and philosophers were repelled by it and developed a significant literature and art in opposition—Jean-Jacques Rousseau and William Blake are particularly to be noted (Roszak, 1972). However, for every one whose work was remembered, there were thousands who simply dropped out, left the cities and sought satisfaction outside the reach of civilization—as farmers, cowboys, shepherds, sailors, fishermen, prospectors, or in the remote wilderness as hunters and trappers. Some joined tribes and became adopted members of Indian, Malay, Polynesian, or African societies—Fletcher Christian of the Mutiny on the H.M.S. Bounty comes to mind. Others disappeared into the then exotic and nonindustrialized civilizations of Asia (Burdick, 1961; Melville, 1961).

What was a mere trickle of "drop outs" in an earlier day, however, became a sizable stream during the 1960s when the young people of the United States, in particular, but also young people from other industrialized countries, became increasingly alienated from their parent societies and sought alternative ways of living. Some attempted to "recolonize" their own cities and for a brief but sparkling period established new communities in such places as the Haight-Ashbury in San Francisco or Greenwich Village in New York. None of these urban communities, however, could survive the combined onslaught of mass media attention, mass tourism, criminals and lawmen. More successful were those who went back to the land. The establishment of rural communes, usually in places considered marginal for mechanized agrobusiness, was accompanied by all the mistakes in farming technique, land use practice, and the management of interpersonal relationships that could be imagined. Nevertheless, the communitarians were willing to learn from their mistakes, and particularly in the United States developed viable communities that were increasingly independent of inputs from technological society. It is difficult to know how many such communities exist in the 1970s, since the successful ones thrive best without publicity, but the number exceeds 2000. Some of these have been highly successful in the development of unconventional energy sources, others have produced bountiful crops from soils or climates considered agriculturally unproductive. As has been noted earlier, with growing recognition of the energy crisis, technological society may turn to its "drop-outs" to learn new skills (Houriet, 1971).

There is an obvious need to reserve certain areas of our planet, land and water, for the practice of nontechnological ways of life. Waters should be reserved for those who would fish by primitive means, and land areas with their wildlife for those who would live by hunting, trapping, and food gathering. Semiarid and mountain grazing lands should be set aside for horse or camel nomadic herdsmen, and other lands of reasonable productivity for the practice of nonmechanized, low-energy-input agriculture. Special attention must be given to the preservation of primitive and more recent nonindustrial arts, crafts, and other skills. The subject is not new, and it is receiving some attention. However, the value of such efforts toward perpetuation of the heritage of human practical knowledge and of alternative ways of life now requires more than casual recognition. International support is called for, not just for the protection of indigenous peoples, but to provide a place for anyone who would choose to live a different kind of life from that offered inside the technocratic web (MacKillop, 1973).

Wildlife Protection

The tragedy represented by the onslaught of industrial civilization against those peoples who sought to live by other ways has only been exceeded by the onslaught against the natural world. The rate at which wild species of plants and animals have become endangered has accelerated with the growth and spread of modern technology, until today it appears that the whole wild world is under threat. Wild people, wild animals, and wild places have gone together, and when one is attacked all are endangered. To finally destroy the fighting spirit of the Plains Indians it was necessary to first destroy their buffalo.

Throughout the history of the earth various species of animals have become extinct. Among the land fauna of past ages it is possible to trace the rise and fall of the giant amphibians to be followed by the age of reptiles. Reptiles reached their peak when the dinosaurs roamed the swamp forests of the Cretaceous era. They disappeared and were replaced by the profusion of mammals that thrived before the Ice Ages of the Pleistocene and Recent epochs. The extinction of species is not new, and past extinctions must be attributed to causes unrelated to man's activities, since humanity did not then exist. However, extinctions of the past were characterized by a slow rate—perhaps millions of years during which dinosaur species slowly disappeared—and by replacement of the past forms by more recently evolved species. Extinction as part of a slow evolutionary process was accompanied by the development of a greater profusion and diversity of life and by the spread of plants and animals into all inhabitable ecological niches on the planet. Extinction of the type being brought about by human activity is of a different sort. It is, for the most part, extinction without replacement leading to an impoverishment of life on earth.

According to some estimates there are at present 4200 species of mammals, 8600 species of birds, around 6000 species of reptiles and 2900 species of amphibians (Curry-Lindahl, 1972). The number of fish species is greater and not as well known. Birds are perhaps better known taxonomically and their classification is more consistent than that of most other groups, yet in 1973 a previously unknown species was discovered in Hawaii. Among mammals taxonomy is still in a state of flux. For example, among wild sheep it is now generally accepted that there are at most 3 species, with a great number of differing forms known as subspecies. A few decades ago most of these subspecies were given the rank of full species by those who first described them. Among plants and invertebrates the number of species living is a matter of guesswork since many new species remain to be discovered or named.

In calculating the rate at which species have become extinct or endangered as a result of human action, it is not of major consequence whether the animal that has become extinct deserves the rank of a species or subspecies since both are dynamic entities in a continuing process of evolution. In either circumstance the life of an area has become correspondingly impoverished. According to Curry-Lindahl, 173 species and subspecies of birds have become extinct during historical time, and of these 157 have become extinct since 1700 A.D. There are 388 more species and subspecies that are now threatened with extinction. Among mammals, at least 112 species and subspecies have become extinct during the historical period, and of these 66 have vanished since 1900 (Goodwin, 1973). At least 275 species or subspecies of mammals are now considered threatened with extinction. These figures are based on the surveillance of species carried out by IUCN (the International Union for Conservation of Nature and Natural Resources) and presented in its Red Data Book of threatened species (Goodwin and Holloway, 1973; Vincent, 1968). This book is now under revision and it is likely that the number of species listed as threatened will be increased in keeping with more recent data.

An Example—the Bovidae

To illustrate the problem of species protection, I will focus for a space on one group of mammals, the Bovidae, the family that includes cattle, sheep, goats, and antelope. Because these animals are large and conspicuous and considered of economic value, they have received more attention than most mammals. Despite this there is much to be learned about them in the wild state. According to my own evaluation of the taxonomic references there are 109 species of Bovidae still in existence in a wild state. Relatively few have become extinct in historic times: the bluebuck of South Africa, a close relative of the relatively abundant blesbuck and bontebuck (and probably of the same species) had been shot out by hunters by 1800; the same fate overtook the rufous gazelle of the Atlas Mountains, which was last seen in 1936, and the Saharan subspecies of the bubal hartebeest, which had vanished by 1923. Various other subspecies have vanished, although the species remain extant. The only clearly defined species that has become extinct is the wild cattle of Europe, the aurochs *(Bos primigenius)* and this exists in genetically modified forms in various European domestic cattle breeds. The aurochs was said to be a forest animal and disappeared along with the extensive forests of Europe. Hunting and competition from domestic livestock contributed to its demise in a wild state. The last wild aurochs were maintained in a forest in Poland until 1627, when the last survivor died.

Although extinction of Bovids in recent years has been minimal, the number that are threatened at the present time is considerable. Ten to 12 species are clearly endangered, and 11 or 12 are in the vulnerable status, meaning that they are approaching the point of endangerment. An additional 11 species are listed as having endangered or rare subspecies, bringing the number of species that are threatened with extinction, to some degree, to 33 or nearly one third of the total number. From information available to IUCN, only 54 species can be considered relatively common, whereas the status of 22 species is somewhat uncertain (we have, for example, no recent information on the status of Chinese species).

If the distribution and habitat of these threatened species is examined, it is found that the Saharan-Arabian desert region, with its surrounding semidesert steppe and dry thornbush savanna (including that of Somalia and Ethiopia) is the home of half, 16, of the threatened forms. The rainforests and monsoon forests of southeast Asia are the location of an additional 8 species, whereas, of the remainder, 5 are high mountain forms. Only 4 species occur in other regions or habitats: two in West African rain forest or savanna, and two in Southern or Central African wetlands or savanna. (No native bovids occur in South America or Australia.) The problems of species conservation among the Bovidae are thus clearly related to those of biotic conservation in general, since it is in the Sahara-Sahel and southwest Asian arid regions that it has been most difficult to achieve conservation of any living resource, and in humid southeast Asia the destruction of the natural environment is now proceeding rapidly. In this region the problems of human conservation are also critical, both in an overall sense and also in relation particularly to endangered ethnic groups.

The endangered species of the Saharan-Sahelian-Arabian region and of high mountains are species that are excessively vulnerable to hunting because of the open habitat that they prefer. Mechanized hunting, using repeating or automatic rifles, and improved transportation have removed the protection once naturally provided to these animals by their keen eyesight, speed, or ability to climb. In the countries in which they occur (which include some of the poorest and some of the richest in the world) it has been most difficult to control poaching or to enforce protective legislation. Only Iran and Israel have put any serious effort into species conservation, and in both of those countries the problem of increasing endangerment seems for the time to have been arrested. The countries of this dry region are also those in which the pressure of the domestic livestock herds on the highly vulnerable forage resource has been most excessive, and in which the effects of periodic drought are felt severely. The effects of the most recent drought (ending in 1973) on the wildlife of this region are as yet little known, but are no doubt severe.

In southeastern Asia, human population increase and destruction of habitat have been greatly accelerated. The tropical forests in this region have suffered a severe onslaught from the introduction of virtually uncontrolled modern logging techniques. The protection once provided by extensive areas of dense forests is being removed, and all wildlife populations have become vulnerable to hunting.

It is of interest to contrast the situation among previously endangered species that have now become relatively secure with those currently threatened. The list of species that have recovered in numbers to a currently safe level includes the American bison, the European bison, the black wildebeest, saiga antelope, mountain goat, musk ox, chamois, and subspecies of the blesbuck (the bontebuck) and of the ibex. It is noteworthy that all of these occupy open habitat (grassland, steppe, savanna, or high mountains) that helps account for their previous depletion. All, however, occur in countries in which the enforcement of antipoaching laws is made relatively easy by public attitudes favorable to wildlife and in which economic standards are sufficiently high that the need for people to seek wild meat for subsistence has been removed. This is, of course, the opposite of the situation that prevails in the countries where most endangered species are found.

Among the endangered species some are now in a critical state. Those for which populations in the wild are probably less than 200 include the tamarau and kouprey (wild cattle of southeast Asia), the Arabian oryx, Swayne's hartebeest, the Zanzibar suni antelope, Pyrenean ibex, Walian ibex, two subspecies of the dama gazelle of northern Africa, and one subspecies of the markhor (a wild goat of southwest Asia). One of these, the Zanzibar suni may well be extinct, and the status of the kouprey in war-ravaged IndoChina is uncertain. The Arabian oryx has been the subject of a massive rescue operation, and its future in captivity, if not in the wild, is reasonably assured.

For all endangered Bovidae there seems to be one important necessity, considering current attitudes toward wildlife, and that is the establishment of one or more well-protected reserves encompassing suitable habitat and populations. Within these reserves habitats must be managed to permit rapid recovery where depletion has taken place, and populations of animals must be carefully guarded. Whenever populations have recovered sufficiently efforts need be made to accomplish a wider distribution within the original range of the species so that it will be less vulnerable to the effects of disease, catastrophe, or a breakdown of the protective regime in any one area. These recommendations are not new. Their implementation depends on the willingness of the peoples and governments concerned to take an active interest in the protection of wild species. Thus far, in most countries, this interest has been lacking.

However, the establishment of parks and reserves along with the enforcement of protective legislation is only a temporary measure for the protection of species. Until humanity recognizes the rights of other species to coexist on planet earth, and takes steps to control its own population increase and exploitation of the earth's resources, no species is secure.

But to consider only the plight of endangered species, dismal though this may be, is to give perhaps too rosy a picture of the status of the world's wildlife. The bison of the American plains is no longer endangered, but nowhere can one find anything approaching the wildlife spectacle that was seen by the Indians and American pioneers when bison, pronghorns, deer, and elk roamed in their tens of millions on the plains and prairies, followed by their companions the wolves and coyotes. The springbuck of South Africa is still relatively numerous, but once the migrating herds covered the landscape from one horizon to another. There are still many great whales in the ocean, but commercial whaling has reduced their numbers to levels far below what existed a century ago, and some species—the blue, humpback, fin, and right whales—are seriously endangered.

There seems no place in the modern world for the wildlife abundance of the past, and in only a few places today can one still gather an appreciation of the sheer mass and drama produced by great numbers of animals congregated. In the Antarctic the original abundance still may be seen, and elsewhere in a few seal or sea bird colonies, or in some of the national parks one can see a sample of the spectacles that were once common.

Efforts to achieve protection of wildlife outside of specially designated areas, as an overall part of a sound land-use policy have not been greatly successful. For the most part, in the absence of any feeling of identity with or respect for wildlife, one must resort to economic arguments. In some places it has been possible to build up a solid economic case for the protection of wild nature. Thus in southern Africa it has been demonstrated that the native wildlife, in areas marginal for agriculture, can bring a greater income from the land than can be obtained from conventional livestock grazing or similar low-intensity land uses (Dasmann, 1964). The income comes from sport hunting, camera safaris, or direct cropping of the animals for sustained yield production of meat, hides, or other products. Recently some land owners have earned much money from the production and sale of live animals for stocking other farms, or for sale to zoos and wildlife parks. A pair of sable antelope, for example, may bring the owner several thousand dollars. The result of this favorable economic balance has been the restoration of wildlife to areas from which they had long ago been exterminated to take the place of, or to share the veld with, the flocks of sheep and herds of cattle. It is a heartening development in South Africa, Southwest Africa, Rhodesia, and Botswana. Unfortunately, the idea has not taken hold in the countries to the north although there have been various demonstrations and pilot projects in East Africa.

One cannot ask too much. An African farmer cannot readily tolerate the presence of lions and elephants in the area where he expects to till his crops, yet a reasonable balance of the less dangerous species outside of the intensively farmed lands would add interest, variety, a change of diet, and some income to the farmers of any region, if a conservation orientation could be instilled. In the past, before the coming of urban-industrial civilization, farmers and herdsmen had learned to live with, to respect, or even to hold in veneration the wild nature that surrounded them. Unfortunately, technocratic man brought with him the concept of a strict separation of man from nature and with that the quantification of all "values" in economic terms. The spirit of the wild could not be quantified and hence was to be ignored.

Habitat Protection

The protection of wild species cannot be carried out without protection of the habitat, the environment to which the species belong. Although it is true that individuals of a species can be protected in a zoo or a botanical garden, it is also true that animals or plants in such locations tend to become behaviorally and, in time, genetically different from their wild forebears. It is extremely doubtful that a third generation zoo tiger would be able to survive in the wild without an extensive period of education, and even that might not be enough.

For the most part, efforts to conserve species have formed a part of a more general effort to conserve biotic communities. This has been accomplished by the formation of national parks and equivalent reserves, as well as a great variety of other protected areas. The idea of setting aside nature reserves seems to be as old as civilization, or perhaps older. For the most part, such early reserves had some special purpose—to make game available for the hunting of the king or nobility, to safeguard wild resources considered necessary for military purposes (e.g., ship's timbers), or because of the religious significance of the area being protected. The concept of setting aside, by governments, of extensive areas of land simply to protect their wildlife and natural communities is one for which the United States is usually given credit. The establishment of Yellowstone National Park in 1872 set a precedent that was soon to be followed by other countries. By 1974 there were nearly 1200 reasonably well-protected national parks or their equivalents, of more than 1000 hectares in extent, located in most countries of the world (IUCN, 1973). If smaller reserves, or partially protected areas are to be considered the number of such reserves must certainly exceed 10,000. However, considered as a percentage of total land area the extent of these reserves is still rather small. Zambia, which has 8 percent of its land in national parks, is a favorable exception to the general rule.

In some countries the national parks are important contributors to the national income. In Kenya income from tourism is the greatest single source of foreign exchange, and the bulk of this is attracted by the wildlife protected in its national parks. In other countries, however, national parks have been protected for other reasons—for cultural values, scientific and educational use, or as stated for Zaire, as part of the country's heritage, and tourism plays no significant role.

Setting aside an area as a national park, however, is far from being all that is needed to guarantee the protection of its natural values. In some countries, Bolivia is an example, the fine system of national parks that exist by law do not exist at all on the ground since they are not protected and are used in just the same way as any other area—for farming, grazing, logging, hunting, mining, or any other purpose. Elsewhere it has been extremely difficult to explain or justify the concept of a national park to the local people. Particularly when they see no economic benefits coming their way they resent being kept out of areas that they have traditionally used. Few governments have realistically tackled the problem of sharing the benefits to be derived from a national park with the people who have suffered by its creation (Gomm, 1974).

The management of a park or a reserve is no simple thing and traditionally it has been a confused and confusing activity. Part of the reason is a failure to have clearly defined purposes to be served in each area protected, and of the ecological requirements that must be met if those purposes are to be served. For example, if we wish to maintain an area as a strict nature reserve, meaning essentially unchanged by human activity, then visitors must be kept out, along with any other activities that could disturb the pristine situation. However, such strict nature reserves are established, in part, for their scientific interest and for this to be realized scientists must be allowed to study them. This places a severe responsibility on the administrator of the reserve since he must see to it that scientists tread "as lightly as angels" while carrying out their studies. Reserves established to protect a particular endangered species or community must be managed in such a way as to maintain conditions favorable for the preservation of that species or community. This may mean interference with natural processes that would go on if the area were left strictly alone (Dasmann, 1973).

Tourism and outdoor recreation provide part of the rationale behind the creation of most national parks, but they can be destructive of the natural values that the park is intended to preserve. Visitors to the Amboseli National Park in Kenya are frequently dismayed by the masses of tourists in their tour buses chasing lions, rhinos, cheetahs, or other spectacular animals around the veld, damaging vegetation and soil in the process as well as interfering with the feeding and resting of the animals. Visitors to Yellowstone and Yosemite have often compared the campgrounds to "rural slums." Control must be exercised over the numbers of tourists visiting a park, and also of the planning and organization of tourist facilities. Although large areas of a park can usually be made available to the wilderness hiker who demands no special facilities, only small corridors can be developed for use of the automobile-bound tourist who also desires special campground facilities.

Reconciling the demands that are placed on national parks has come to require the work of a special kind of expert, the ecologically oriented park planner. Without planning, national parks can rapidly deteriorate under present conditions of park use and with existing attitudes toward nature.

Unfortunately, national parks today are forced to serve purposes for which they were never intended. In addition to being prestige items that tourists wish to chalk up on their lists of things to do, they are forced to provide for a kind of mass recreation that could far better be served by areas of less value for nature conservation, and preferably located close to urban centers. With proper planning for community outdoor recreation much of the pressure on the parks could be removed. But unfortunately, this brings up another dilemma. If the parks did not attract masses of visitors, would the government appropriate money for their protection and management? The answer seems to be no. Hence, park managers struggle as best they can to keep the visiting hordes happy while somehow, at the same time, protecting wild nature.

It is difficult to be optimistic about the future of nature conservation despite the many gains that have been chalked up by conservationists in the past century. In the face of growing human populations, the ever-spreading impact of urban-industrial growth on the countryside, the generally destructive and uncontrolled forms of land use that characterize most countries, and the increase of levels of pollution, the outlook for maintaining natural diversity is not bright.

To add to the problem, nature conservationists appear to be an unusually disunited lot who spend more time fighting among themselves than they do addressing the job to be done. This seems to be a problem with any movement that seeks to change human attitudes or to provide leadership to a reluctant majority of mankind. But in conservation, which should provide a banner behind which people could rally, it is particularly disturbing to see continuing interne-cine warfare. How this can be solved at the present time escapes me, since organizations that are intended to bring conservation groups together such as the Natural Resources Council of America, or the International Union for Conservation of Nature and Natural Resources, seem only to provide arenas within which old battles are fought out and new feuds started.

References

Barkataki, S. 1971. The hill tribes of Assam. *Ecologist, 1*: 4–7.

Bates, H. W. 1910. *The naturalist on the river Amazon.* Everyman's Library, Dutton, New York, 1969 ed.

Brown, Dee. 1970. *Bury my heart at Wounded Knee.* Bantam Books, New York, 1972 ed.

Burdick, Eugene. 1961. *The blue of Capricorn.* Fawcett, Greenwich, Connecticut.

Castaneda, Carlos. 1972. *Journey to Ixtlan.* Simon & Schuster, New York.

Chatwin, Bruce. 1970. The last hunters of the Sahara. The Nemadi of Mauritania. *Ecologist, 1*: 30–33.

Curry-Lindahl, Kai. 1972. *Let them live.* Wm. Morrow, New York.

Dasmann, R. F. 1964. *African game ranching.* Pergamon, Oxford.

Dasmann, R. F. 1972. *Environmental conservation,* 3rd ed. John Wiley, New York.

Dasmann, R. F. 1972. Towards a system for classifying natural regions of the world and their representation by national parks and reserves. *Biological Conservation* 4 (4): 247–255.

Dasmann, R. F. 1973. *Classification and use of protected natural and cultural areas.* IUCN Occasional Paper No. 4, IUCN, Morges.

Deloria, Vine, Jr. 1969. *Custer died for your sins.* Avon Books, New York (1970 ed.).

Ecologist. 1972. A blueprint for survival. *Ecologist 2* (1): 1–43.

Fanon, Frantz. 1961. *The wretched of the earth.* Penguin Books, Harmondsworth (1971 ed.).

Gomm, Roger. 1974. The elephant men. *Ecologist 4*: 53–57.

Goodwin, H. and J. 1973. *List of mammals which have become extinct or are possibly extinct since 1600.* IUCN Occasional Paper No. 8, Morges, Switzerland.

Goodwin, Harry and Colin Holloway. 1973. *Red Data Book.* Volume 1: *Mammalia.* IUCN, Morges, Switzerland.

Houriet, Robert. 1971. *Getting back together.* Abacus, London (1973 ed.).

IUCN. 1973. *United Nations List of National Parks and Equivalent Reserves.* IUCN, Morges. (See also earlier editions.)

Keith, Shirley. 1972. The AmerIndian tragedy. *Ecologist 2*: 13–22.

MacKillop, Andrew. 1973. Technological alternatives. *New Scientist, 60* (873): 549–551.

Marriott, A. and C. K. Rachlin. 1968. *American Indian mythology.* Mentor, New American Library, New York (1972 ed.).

Melville, Herman. 1961. *Typee.* Bantam Books, New York.

Moorehead, Alan. 1966. *The fatal impact.* Penguin (1968 ed.), Harmondsworth, U. K.

Neel, James V. 1970. Lessons from a "primitive" people. *Science, 170:* 815–822.

Neihardt, John G. 1932. *Black Elk speaks.* Pocket Books, New York, 1972 ed.

O'Shaughnessy, Hugh. 1973. *What future for the Amerindians of South America?* Minority Rights Report 15. Minority Rights Group, London.

Roszak, Theodore. 1972. *Where the wasteland ends.* Doubleday, New York.

Sauer, Carl O. 1964. *The early Spanish Main.* University Calif. Press, Berkeley.

Smith, Anthony. 1971. *Mato Grosso.* Dutton, New York.

Smith, Nigel J. 1971. *The potential impact of Brazil's Transamazon highway on fauna and aboriginal populations.* University California Department Geography, mimeo.

Snyder, Gary. 1972. Four changes. *Sources* (ed. T. Roszak) Harper & Row, Colophon, New York, pp. 373–388.

Swift, Jeremy. 1972. *Pastoral nomadism as a form of land use; the Tuareg of the Adrar n Iforas (Mali).* University Sussex, United Kingdom, mimeo.

Vincent, Jack. 1968. *Red Data Book.* Volume 2, *Aves.* IUCN, Morges.

Waller, Robert. 1971. Out of the garden of Eden. *New Scientist,* 2 Sept., pp. 528–530.

Wilkinson, Richard G. 1973. Progress to poverty. *Ecologist* 3 (9): 342–347.

chapter eight

The Conservation Alternative

"If I could turn you on, if I could drive you out of your wretched mind, if I could tell you I would let you know."

R. D. Laing, *The bird of paradise*

The Existing Crisis

For those who have read the preceding chapters, it is hardly necessary to restate the necessity for finding alternatives to the resource-consuming, energy-wasting, land-destroying, biosphere-shattering way of life that characterizes the advanced industrial civilizations, and their followers in the developing nations. Nevertheless, it may be worthwhile to review the major problems.

1.   Civilization today lives always on the brink, and uses a high percentage of its energy and resources to prepare for total war. On what we call a "small" scale, which is not small at all to the millions who are caught up in it, wars break out continually in Indochina, Bangladesh, the Middle East, Iraq, Portuguese Africa, Sudan, and so on. The record since the Second World War has been one of almost continuous localized wars. However, the major powers constantly prepare for a war that would be totally destructive, that would kill hundreds of millions of people, destroy civilization, and perhaps make the earth

149

unfit for life. That this is madness, and that civilization as we know it is mad need hardly be restated.

2.   Civilization today has brought great material wealth to a minority of the world's people, while leaving the majority in desperate poverty. Since those in control make only feeble efforts to change this situation, and many of these seem only to make matters worse, the distance between rich and poor grows greater. When this is added to the continued existence of military machines and the capacity for totally destructive wars it creates a condition too perilous to be allowed to persist. Even without the threat of war, the conditions that exist are intolerable and can lead only to disaster.

3.   The world today is beset by a level of human population that in 1974 approaches 4 billion people and is growing at a rate of 2 percent per year. Regardless of any breakthroughs that may occur in new sources of energy, minerals, and food this rate of population growth cannot continue. However, it can only be halted by either increasing the rate of mortality, or by limiting birth rates. Since in the greater part of the world the incentive for limiting births does not appear to exist, we must assume that populations will increase toward a period when millions or hundred millions of people will die from starvation or some combinaton of malnutrition and disease. This is an intolerable condition.

4.   Technology has apparently grown out of human control and is oriented toward an economy of consumption and waste within which the only major goal appears to be continued growth, which is known as progress. The rate of growth of this economy cannot long be sustained by known or reasonably predictable sources of energy and raw materials. Furthermore the economy appears to have reached a point of diminishing returns in its capacity to provide human satisfaction in any other form than crass consumption of more and more goods.

5.   Pollution of the environment is reaching ever higher and more dangerous levels, and efforts at pollution control have not been generally effective, in part because of the continued increase in population and economic growth based on waste, in part because pollution is approached as a separate phenomenon from the system that produces it, and in part because the desire to increase economic productivity in the short run overrides consideration of long-term consequences.

6.   Destruction of the life-support systems of the biosphere, based on animal and plant life and the soils and waters that support them, is continuing at an accelerating rate, not only because of pollution, but particularly because of ruthless methods for extracting greater quantities of living resources and industrial raw materials.

Without further listing or elaboration, it should be apparent that the title of Chapter 1 "Present Trends Cannot Continue" is only a mild statement of the situation. The life destructive trends now operative in the world must be halted and reversed. New ways of living on earth that can be permanently sustained must be found. The search for these ways cannot be long postponed, since it is the present generation of people on which "the hard rains are going to fall." The argument concerning "why worry about posterity?" no longer holds. We are the posterity they were arguing about. Is it not fortunate that some people, however small a minority, have started the search?

Steps Toward a Conservation Alternative

It is not within my capability to write *A Blueprint for Survival* of the world. However, some tasks that must be undertaken are obvious. These will be listed in two categories: those in which the principal action must be taken by governments and where the individual can only help by working through conservation organizations, or, less effectively, alone to see to it that his representatives in government address themselves to these issues and come up with the right answers. The individual can also play a role locally, in those areas over which he may have some influence or control, to see to it that the appropriate recommendations are carried out. The second category is one in which governments may not be willing to play a positive role in the immediate future, but in which individuals can act directly through "voting with their feet" or changing their life styles to accomplish the needed actions. In listing these various tasks, the ones that can be accomplished more quickly, or with the least difficulty will be first discussed, the more difficult ones later.

Actions To Be Taken Primarily at the Government Level

1. *Conservation of wild nature.*   We must put a stop wherever possible to the destruction of the world's wild places and wildlife. This means, within the United States, definition, proclamation, and protection of all of those wilderness areas that remain and are not yet included within the wilderness system. It further means extension of the system of national parks and biological reserves to protect, not only the scenic and spectacular areas, but also those more ordinary but representative areas of every kind of biotic community. At the international level it means support by the wealthy nations for the establishment of an international network of national parks, biological reserves, and various kinds of cultural reserves. Practical steps would include ratification and support of the World Heritage Convention, which is now held open for signature in Unesco and provides for funds to assist poor nations in protecting their natural and cultural heritage. Other steps would include the provision of funds and technical assistance for the establishment of the system of biosphere reserves called for in the Man and the Biosphere Programme of Unesco. Support for international nongovernmental agencies such as the International Union for Conservation of Nature and Natural Resources (IUCN) and its partner organization the World Wildlife Fund will help accomplish these objectives.

Within the United States, as in other countries, it is particularly important to do away with the special privileges that certain groups may have, and most notably the mining industry, in relation to wilderness areas and other protected areas. These natural areas must remain free from exploitation so that they can continue to serve as reservoirs of wild creatures and sources of inspiration to those people who will visit them without seeking to modify them.

2. *Islands, Mountains and Fragile Areas.*   Particular care must be provided to maintain the biotic communities of oceanic islands, high mountains, estuaries and coastal coral reefs, as well as other unusually fragile and easily disrupted ecosystems. This may in some cases involve the establishment of national parks or biological reserves in these areas, but in other instances it will involve modifying land-use practices to guard against destructive effects. Equal care should be given to protect the rights, and ways of life, of those indigenous and traditional societies that still exist in islands, high mountains, and other fragile areas where these still represent means for balancing human use with the long-term survival of wild nature, or are otherwise in ecological balance with their environments.

3. *Balanced Land Use.*   For those areas already modified by human activity and necessary for the production of food, fiber, or other renewable resources, but still in a relatively wild state, programs of management based on the principles of sustained yield must be instituted. This is essential if such areas are to continue to supply forest products, range forage, fisheries, other wild animal products, fresh water, and other materials useful to man. Such land must not be converted to uses that will have less value over the long-term, regardless of any immediate gain to be made, nor to uses that cannot be sustained.

Specifically this means that estuaries, marshes, and other wetlands needed for the maintenance of aquatic life must not be polluted, filled in, drained, dredged, or otherwise destroyed. It means that forests are not to be logged, or otherwise exploited, in ways that will impair their long-term productivity, nor should they be converted to other nonsustainable uses. It means that rangelands must not be overgrazed or trampled to a degree from which recovery is difficult or impossible, and that watersheds, regardless of their vegetation or the appropriate form of land use, be managed in ways that sustain production of clear water for streams, lakes and reservoirs.

4. *Ocean resources.*   Administration and protection of the oceans and their resources, including the sea bottoms, outside of national territorial waters, must be placed in the hands of an international body that will have power to enforce its authority. This could be of the nature of *The Ocean Regime* proposed by Borgese (1970), or some equivalent agency. Income derived from the exploitation of ocean resources should be shared among all nations, and not just the coastal states. Exploitation of the oceans, their living resources, and of the sea bottoms with their mineral wealth must be carried out in such

ways and at such levels that their long-term productivity is not impaired. This applies equally to areas under national as well as under international jurisdiction. Severe penalties must be imposed against those activities that result in serious pollution of the oceans, and the means for enforcing these penalties must be provided to the international oceans agency.

5. *Protection of "peripheral" peoples.* Protection must be given at international and national levels to those peoples who still practice preindustrial ways of life, outside of the prevailing technocratic societies—hunter-gatherer-fishermen, nomadic pastoralists, preindustrial agriculturalists, and the like. Such peoples who have traditionally occupied lands, long before nation-states were created, must have their rights to their lands, or the resources they have traditionally used for survival, legally recognized. Within their lands they should be allowed full autonomy, with the freedom to change or develop at their own pace and in directions of their choosing. Attention must also to be given to providing lands for the specific use of those who seek to return to preindustrial ways of life, and to leaving these without interference from advanced technological societies.

6. *Transportation systems.* Replacement of energy-and-materials-wasting systems of transportation by energy-efficient, mass-transportation systems must be carried out as quickly as possible. For the present time, rail and ship transport should be encouraged by all means, except where more efficient systems can be devised. Money that is now expended toward the building or widening of highways for automobile and truck transport must be channeled into other systems that can be operated at less energy cost. Air and automobile transport, including trucking, must be progressively deemphasized. During the period when efficient public-transportation systems are being constructed, automobiles and trucks should be converted as quickly as possible to make use of fuels that are either renewable or relatively cheap and abundant, or to engines that make much more efficient use of fossil fuels than those currently in use. Mass tourism by air, which has presented a serious drain on energy resources, as well as being a growing source of environmental and social disruption, should be discouraged, while bearing in mind the disruptive effects this will have on the economy of countries that are heavily dependent on income from tourism, and taking steps to provide alternative sources of support for these people.

7. *Economic development.* Major engineering programs intended for the economic development of the Third World, or for marginal areas within the other two "worlds" should only proceed where the relation between total costs (economic, social, ecological) and total benefits, over the long run, are clearly in favor of benefits, and the costs do not include irreparable losses to the natural environment. In no case should such developments take place without the agreement of the peoples who occupy the areas to be modified.

Programs of international aid and technical assistance organizations—the United Nations, World Bank, regional development banks, bilateral aid organizations—should be examined with a view to deemphasize massive and spectacular engineering developments, and provide direct assistance at the "grass roots" level. Programs that are based on the application of low-impact or intermediate technology, which favor the development or improvement of small, self-reliant communities, and that provide direct assistance to the poor peasant and the local craftsmen, should take precedence over those that promise benefits "filtering down from the top" from expenditures intended to increase the gross national product through developing the local technocracy.

8. *War and peace.*   A massive effort must be carried out to reduce and eventually eliminate national expenditures for military purposes. Although it may appear risky in a world armed to the teeth for any one nation to disarm, bold steps are required in view of the growing seriousness of the situation. If, for example, the United States was to announce to the world that it would, slowly, step by step, dismantle its war machine, and each year turn over the money saved for direct use in international aid and technical assistance to poor countries, the example could be a precedent other nations could scarcely resist following.

Various proposals have been made for the creation of an international "peace-keeping" force. Admittedly the United Nations today cannot be described as a just or impartial organization, but within its framework, or outside, it should be possible to establish a nonpartisan, unbiased, and responsible group that could be charged with a peace-keeping mission. Such an organization would require both the necessary military power and impeccable international prestige if it were to function effectively. Its existence alone could be sufficient to put a halt to armed conflicts between nations. Its presence would bring to an end the need for anything other than local peace-keeping forces at the national level.

It should be noted that all of the above recommendations can be carried out, although it is doubtful that they will be, without any marked changes in the present structure of society. International bureaucracies, the domination of nation-states over their internal affairs, and the world's "megamachines" need not be greatly changed, nor the ways in which technocracy operates seriously modified. It is not in tended that the above list is exhaustive or comprehensive, any more than that this book covers all areas of conservation. It is believed, however, that the above actions, or some improved versions of them, are essential for long-term survival of humanity. The changes to be recommended at the individual level are more comprehensive and will ultimately result in the dismantling of the technocratic societies of the world.

Actions To Be Taken Primarily at the Individual Level

There should be no doubt that the next 25 years will be difficult and in many parts of the world, for many people, they will be at times sheer hell. There seems to be no way in which disasters and catastrophes can be avoided, but with a major effort their effects can be minimized and their lessons can be made apparent if nations are willing to work toward this end. The next 25 years, however, will provide what may be the last chance on earth to create a sane, viable human society based on the employment of high technology. What is required is no less than a break up of the "megamachine" into components that can be operated as part of an ecologically sound, human-scaled economy. This will not be done quickly, and must be carried out skillfully if we are to avoid serious breakdowns in the total society. For example, we cannot immediately abandon the energy-depleting monocultures that at present supply most of the world's grain. Instead we must build up an alternative agricultural system that will slowly replace (but not too slowly), and take over from the existing system. Because civilization as it exists today is scarcely able to change itself, the immediate direction must be "to build a new society within the shell of the old"—to create viable, and eventually self-sustaining units and networks that can assimilate the necessary functions of the technocratic society.

9. *Decentralization of society.* Virtually everyone who has examined the existing world situation from an ecological viewpoint is led to recommend a program of decentralization. We have already considered the recommendations of Lewis Mumford, Odum, *The Blueprint for Survival* and many others. Two additional viewpoints follow. Isaac Asimov, biochemist, futurist, and technological optimist has examined the long term future of society, to the year 3000. He assumes that nuclear fusion power will solve all energy problems—but only providing that we tackle the reduction of human population, control pollution, and turn away from further preparations for war. With those provisions he sees a world with a population of one billion people and a highly advanced technology. However, "Long before 3000 the city may have withered as a human institution and people will live in relatively small scattered communities. . . . Nations will exist as marks on a map. But there will, effectively, be a world government. . . ."

By contrast, economist E. F. Schumacher cautions against the risks of developing nuclear power any further and recommends instead the employment of solar energy and its derivatives. Use of these power sources virtually forces decentralization. He states: "It may seem surprising that a consideration of energy "policy has taken us 'back to the soil' and thus 'back to nature'. But this is quite inevitable if we wish to move from the surface of the problem to its root. . . . the challenge presented by the energy problem is one of developing a new life-style—a development which logically and inevitably must begin with a change of man's relation to the soil of which he is a product and which alone sustains his life."

It is recommended therefore that we turn our immediate attention to the establishment of decentralized communities based on ecologically sound, organically based agricultural practices, and on local technologies using energy sources that can be sustained. Raw materials of a nonrenewable nature must be used sparingly and where possible reused or recycled within these local communities. Steps in this direction already have been taken in various communes or other intentional communities based on organic agriculture and alternative energy supplies. Most of these, however, have been located in agriculturally marginal lands. It is time that they move into the better farming lands with higher, sustainable productivity.

If we move now, while energy and resources are available, a return to organic agriculture and decentralized communities will not mean, except where this is desired, a return to a "primitive" way of life. Instead, the best products, tools and equipment available in technological society should be used to create a sustainable agriculture and local technology. For example, a combination of solar heating of homes and other buildings, and perhaps of solar-energy electrical generation; of wind power for electrical generation, pumping, and other purposes; of methane generators using organic wastes to produce fuel and fertilizer, including fuel for transportation; the development where practical of small-scale hydroelectric power systems, or or geothermal energy-generating systems can be used to maintain necessary household heating and lighting, to power farm machinery, and to supply the energy needs of local factories, workshops, and small scale industries. Such a move would end the steady and rapid drain on depleting fossil fuel resources, reserving the remaining supplies for those purposes for which they are most essential, and would end any need for massive development of a high-risk, nuclear-power network.

Furthermore, there is no reason to believe that there will be a decreased output from organic farming and gardening compared to the high-energy-input agriculture that now dominates. In Switzerland the cooperative established originally by Dr. Hans Müller now numbers more than 700 farms supplying produce to the Biotta health food company and to Migros, a major Swiss supermarket chain. None of these farms use chemical fertilizers, pesticides, or herbicides, yet their yields, in some cases, are twice the national average and the cost of their products is no higher than the chemically produced crops from other areas (Bunyard, 1973).

Decentralized communities need not be based on agriculture, although organic gardening in any community will remove the need for much of the expensive, energy-wasting transport of foods that could as well be produced locally. One can visualize an extensive network of forest industry communities, pastoral communities, fishing communities, as well as those based around special crafts, educational institutes, religious organizations, or other activities. Furthermore, such communities, through bringing people into direct involvement with the natural, or managed, biotic communities from which they obtain their livelihood, are likely to remove much of the tendency toward destructive exploitation of resources.

Revitalizing the small towns and villages, not only through bringing people back to work on the land, but through the decentralization of industry would relieve urban congestion and reverse the trend toward growth of megalopolis. In turn the cities could be opened up and humanized, with emphasis on the development of viable neighborhoods within which people can relate as members of communities. Such urban neighborhoods could in turn develop a high degree of self-sufficiency in energy use, production of food in urban gardens, recycling of wastes, and so forth. Certain activities, such as foreign trade and commerce, and those forms of production that are more efficiently handled in a centralized way, would necessarily be based in urbanized areas.

Although one could hope for encouragement of such developments from government, there is no indication at the present time that the mass society is prepared to move in the direction of decentralization. At best one can hope for some assistance and cooperation from such departments as Agriculture, Housing and Urban Development, Health Education, and Welfare, the Environmental Protection Agency, and their state and local equivalents. At least one could get by with a benign indifference on the part of the technocracy, and hope to avoid opposition and hostility. For the present, progress is most likely to be made by those individuals and groups who "opt out of the system" and come together to form decentralized communities.

For those who wish to make a start, there is now far more information than was available to the commune movement of the 1960s, along with many successful models that can be followed. Organic farming is of course as old a practice as agriculture itself, although much has been forgotten in recent decades. The revival of interest in organic agriculture owes much to the work of Sir Albert Howard, whose *An agricultural testament* provides a good introduction to the subject. For practical experience with organic farming in America such publications as *The Last Whole Earth Catalog,* and the periodical *Mother Earth News* open up whole vistas of practical information on the skills needed for developing farming and local technology. In the United Kingdom the periodicals *Ecologist and Resurgence* play a similar role, whereas the Low Impact Technology group in Cornwall and the Intermediate Technology Development group in London are sources of information on small-scale technology suitable for decentralized communities.

10.   *Population growth.*   The establishment of decentralized communities in itself will bring recognition of the need to halt growth of population and of economies. By bringing more people into close touch with the processes that support life, the limits of the environment will become more obvious. Furthermore, by removing the expectation that it is the responsibility of the authorities, of big government or big industry to "do something about the situation," people will become aware of their personal responsibilities. In a true community, moreover, the rearing of children becomes a process in which all can, to some degree, participate. The need to avoid the problems of the "only

child" vanishes, as would some of the urge to reproduce just for the joy of seeing young people growing up.

Nevertheless there will remain important roles for government in publicizing the dangers of overpopulation and the reality of environmental limits, and in developing a national policy opposed to continuing population growth. There is a need also for governments to make freely available the information and means by which unwanted pregnancies can be avoided, or terminated.

It is not possible to predict the level of population at which optimum conditions for each individual would be likely to prevail. However, it is likely to be a much lower level than now prevails. Zero population growth, therefore, is only a beginning goal. It probably should be replaced in most countries by a negative growth rate aiming at a more optimum population level. Thus the two-child, or replacement, family should be considered not the optimum, but the maximum, number of children toward which a couple should aspire.

11. *Development of self.* The decentralization of society will not in itself restore either a sense of community nor a feeling of unity with nature and respect for the environment. People have been badly warped by the training they have received in childhood and beyond in order to fit them for work in technocratic society and for obedience to its rules. Characteristics of aggressiveness, competitiveness, and above all alienation from one's self and others are found in far too many of us. George Leonard has pointed out that in order to function in Civilization one must be properly equipped with a "neurosis/disease/discontent." Nor would a return to the spirit of the small town and village of the old, rural American provide any renewed sense of freedom and community. One must remember that young people, and those not young, fled in droves from the restrictions of town and village, seeking some sense of personal liberty in the anonymity of the city.

Technocratic society and its predecessors have been particularly cruel in their treatment of the two sexes. By prescribing a limited role for women, and another for men, society has not only severely crippled women in their development of self, but unnecessarily handicapped them in every field of endeavor. Men on the other hand, separated from their families by their work, have been further burdened by being forced to demonstrate their "masculinity" and *machismo* at every turn and virtually forbidden to express any positive feelings or the more tender emotions.

To regain a sense of community it will be necessary to change the system of child rearing and education, to play down sex differences and eliminate traditional sex roles, other than those prescribed by biology. In place of little boys and little girls—each with their prescribed rules for permissible behavior, we should raise little people who will grow into their potential as human beings. This in turn will involve the liberalization of attitudes toward sexual behavior and a disappearance of those self-destroying restrictions that forced people on the one hand to flee from the prurient eyes of their hometown neighbors,